AL BLYTH

Al Blyth studied Econometrics at Bristol and LSE, before
working as a research economist at the Institute for Fiscal
Studies. In 2006 he was awarded Soho Theatre's Westminster
Prize, for his play *Furnace Four*. He was selected for the Paines
Plough Future Perfect scheme in 2008, and won Channel 4's
4Talent Prize for Dramatic Writing the same year.

Al's TV show *The Rook*, a supernatural spy thriller based on
the novel by Daniel O'Malley, premiered on the cable network
Starz in 2019.

The Haystack is Al's debut full-length play. Previous short
pieces produced in the UK include *Reality* and *The Poet of
Elswick Park* (RSC/Live Theatre); *Under My Skin* (Paines
Plough/Òran Mór); *Community Payback* (RIFT Theatre);
The Abolition of Death (RSC) and *The Hag of Hyde Park*
(Paines Plough/Shakespeare's Globe).

Other Titles in this Series

Annie Baker
THE ANTIPODES
THE FLICK
JOHN

Mike Bartlett
ALBION
BULL
GAME
AN INTERVENTION
KING CHARLES III
SNOWFLAKE
VASSA *after* Gorky
WILD

Jez Butterworth
THE FERRYMAN
JERUSALEM
JEZ BUTTERWORTH PLAYS: ONE
JEZ BUTTERWORTH PLAYS: TWO
MOJO
THE NIGHT HERON
PARLOUR SONG
THE RIVER
THE WINTERLING

Caryl Churchill
BLUE HEART
CHURCHILL PLAYS: THREE
CHURCHILL PLAYS: FOUR
CHURCHILL PLAYS: FIVE
CHURCHILL: SHORTS
CLOUD NINE
DING DONG THE WICKED
A DREAM PLAY *after* Strindberg
DRUNK ENOUGH TO SAY I LOVE YOU?
ESCAPED ALONE
FAR AWAY
GLASS. KILL. BLUEBEARD'S
        FRIENDS. IMP.
HERE WE GO
HOTEL
ICECREAM
LIGHT SHINING IN
        BUCKINGHAMSHIRE
LOVE AND INFORMATION
MAD FOREST
A NUMBER
PIGS AND DOGS
SEVEN JEWISH CHILDREN
THE SKRIKER
THIS IS A CHAIR
THYESTES *after* Seneca
TRAPS

Fiona Doyle
ABIGAIL
COOLATULLY
DELUGE
THE STRANGE DEATH OF JOHN DOE

Ifeyinwa Frederick
THE HOES

Matt Hartley
DEPOSIT
EYAM
HERE I BELONG
LAST LETTERS HOME
SIXTY FIVE MILES

Vicky Jones
THE ONE
TOUCH

Anna Jordan
CHICKEN SHOP
FREAK
POP MUSIC
THE UNRETURNING
WE ANCHOR IN HOPE
YEN

Lucy Kirkwood
BEAUTY AND THE BEAST
        with Katie Mitchell
BLOODY WIMMIN
THE CHILDREN
CHIMERICA
HEDDA *after* Ibsen
IT FELT EMPTY WHEN THE
        HEART WENT AT FIRST BUT
        IT IS ALRIGHT NOW
LUCY KIRKWOOD PLAYS: ONE
MOSQUITOES
NSFW
TINDERBOX
THE WELKIN

Mike Lew
TEENAGE DICK

Charley Miles
BLACKTHORN
DAUGHTERHOOD
THERE ARE NO BEGINNINGS

Amy Ng
ACCEPTANCE
SHANGRI-LA

Chinonyerem Odimba
AMONGST THE REEDS
PRINCESS & THE HUSTLER
UNKNOWN RIVERS

Sam Steiner
KANYE THE FIRST
LEMONS LEMONS LEMONS
        LEMONS LEMONS
A TABLE TENNIS PLAY
YOU STUPID DARKNESS!

Jack Thorne
2ND MAY 1997
BUNNY
BURYING YOUR BROTHER IN
        THE PAVEMENT
A CHRISTMAS CAROL *after* Dickens
THE END OF HISTORY…
HOPE
JACK THORNE PLAYS: ONE
JUNKYARD
LET THE RIGHT ONE IN
        after John Ajvide Lindqvist
MYDIDAE
THE SOLID LIFE OF SUGAR WATER
STACY & FANNY AND FAGGOT
WHEN YOU CURE ME
WOYZECK *after* Büchner

Phoebe Waller-Bridge
FLEABAG

Alexandra Wood
THE EMPTY QUARTER
THE HUMAN EAR
THE INITIATE
MERIT
THE TYLER SISTERS
UNBROKEN

Al Blyth

THE
HAYSTACK

NICK HERN BOOKS

London

www.nickhernbooks.co.uk

A Nick Hern Book

The Haystack first published in Great Britain in 2020 as a paperback original by Nick Hern Books Limited, The Glasshouse, 49a Goldhawk Road, London W12 8QP

The Haystack copyright © 2020 Al Blyth

Al Blyth has asserted his right to be identified as the author of this work

Cover image by SWD

Designed and typeset by Nick Hern Books, London
Printed in Great Britain by Mimeo Ltd, Huntingdon, Cambridgeshire PE29 6XX

A CIP catalogue record for this book is available from the British Library

ISBN 978 1 84842 908 6

Woodland
CARBON
www.woodlandcarbon.co.uk
NICK HERN BOOKS
Printed on Carbon Captured paper

The Haystack was first performed at Hampstead Theatre, London, on 31 January 2020. The cast was as follows:

DENISE	Lucy Black
NEIL	Oliver Johnstone
CORA	Rona Morison
ZEF	Enyi Okoronkwo
HANNAH	Sarah Woodward
ROB	Oli Higginson (*Video Performer*)
AMEERA	Sirine Saba (*Video Performer*)

Director	Roxana Silbert
Designer	Tom Piper
Costume	Emma Cains
Lighting	Rick Fisher
Sound Design & Composition	Ben & Max Ringham
Video	Duncan McLean
Movement	Wayne Parsons
Casting	Juliet Horsley CDG

Acknowledgements

For background research:

GCHQ by Richard J. Aldrich

Chatter by Patrick Radden Keefe

No Place to Hide by Glenn Greenwald

The Snowden Files by Luke Harding

Citizenfour (documentary) by Laura Poitras

The Annual Reports of the Interception of Communications Commissioner

The Interception of Communications Code of Practice published by the Home Office.

'Inside GCHQ: Welcome to Cheltenham's cottage industry', (*The Register*, May 2013) by Bob Dorman

'GCHQ: inside the top secret world of Britain's biggest spy agency', (*Guardian*, August 2013) by Nick Hopkins, Julian Borger and Luke Harding

Little Brother by Cory Doctorow

Reporting on the Edward Snowden leaks by the *Guardian* and *The Intercept* provided rich sources of both information and inspiration.

Thanks to Martin Bright and James Ball for illuminating conversations about the work of investigative journalists, and the handling of whistleblowers.

I'd like to acknowledge the work of Privacy International, Liberty, Amnesty International, the American Civil Liberties Union, and Human Rights Watch. Their lawsuits against GCHQ (and the NSA) led to open hearings of the Investigatory Powers Tribunal in 2014, at which I spent several eye-opening days.

Cora's article on pages 28–29 draws on Olivia Laing's 'The Future of Loneliness' (*Guardian*, April 2015, excerpted from her book, *The Lonely City*), the Kaiser Family Foundation's 'International Survey on Loneliness and Social Isolation', and the BBC's Loneliness Experiment.

A.B.

For Sam,
who knows more about me than anyone should have to

Characters

DENISE, *forties, Home Affairs editor,* Guardian
NEIL, *late twenties, Technical Intelligence Analyst, GCHQ*
ZEF, *twenties, Technical Intelligence Analyst, GCHQ*
HANNAH, *forties, Deputy Director, Counter-Terrorism
    Directorate, GCHQ*
CORA, *late twenties, journalist,* Guardian
AMEERA, *late thirties, divorced Saudi Princess, seeking
    asylum in London*

SUPPORTING CHARACTERS
(*potentially doubled by main cast*)
ROB, *twenty-five, junior advertising executive*
DAVE, *paramedic, London Ambulance Service*
RACHEL, *paramedic, London Ambulance Service*

*This text went to press before the end of rehearsals and so may
differ slightly from the play as performed.*

ACT ONE

Darkness.

A computer cursor blips into life, projected against the back wall. Blinking silently.

A circle of light fades up on DENISE *(smartly dressed), standing, looking out at the audience. She waits. Nothing happens. The cursor blinks. Finally she speaks –*

DENISE. I'm here.

*The cursor zips to the right, typing out: '**I'm here.**'*

DENISE *waits. Nothing happens.*

Hello? I'm here. We said eight o'clock.

*Again the cursor zips across, typing out her words: '**Hello? I'm here. We said eight o'clock.**'*

DENISE *waits. Nothing happens. The cursor continues to tap out* DENISE*'s words.*

I've set everything up exactly as you asked. This is a brand-new computer, purchased off the shelf this afternoon – using cash, not credit card – from a shop I chose at random. I'm running Tails from a USB stick. I'm using wifi at the house of an acquaintance of a friend of a friend. I've authenticated the… thing, the encryption thing, with the phrase we agreed. I'm here, I've done what you asked. Are you there?

DENISE *waits. Nothing happens.*

NEIL *appears in his own circle of light, across the stage. He wears jeans and a hoodie, the hood pulled low over his face.*

NEIL. The red button.

The cursor changes colour – in green text, it types out the words NEIL *spoke ('**The red button.**') For the next few moments,* DENISE*'s words will project as white text,* NEIL*'s words as green text.*

DENISE. What?

NEIL. The red button. Bottom right-hand corner of your screen.

DENISE. Shit. Forgot. One second.

The projected text and blinking cursor disappear. The lights on DENISE *and* NEIL *change colour – acquiring a reddish tinge.* DENISE *and* NEIL *continue to face the audience as they speak to each other.*

It says 'private chat enabled'. That's right, isn't it – we're secure now?

NEIL. More than we were.

DENISE. That doesn't sound reassuring.

NEIL. Our messages are encrypted in transit. But encryption's irrelevant if the end point is compromised.

DENISE. Can we speak freely, or can't we?

Beat. NEIL *considers his answer.*

NEIL. We can try.

DENISE. Before we start, I have to ask: why me? This is a long way outside my usual 'beat'…

NEIL. I know.

DENISE. Plenty of journalists who cover this stuff for a living. Some of them work for me.

NEIL. It has to be you.

DENISE. Why?

NEIL. Because she liked you.

DENISE. Who?

NEIL. Cora. (*Then.*) Cora Preece.

The name shocks DENISE.

DENISE. Do you have information? About what happened to Cora?

NEIL. I think it's probable that I know more about Cora Preece than anyone else on this planet.

DENISE. And what do you want in return? How much – ?

NEIL. I don't want money.

DENISE. Then what do you want?

NEIL pulls down the hood, uncovering his face. He looks up.

NEIL. I want to confess.

The sound of a roaring car engine booms out – as the circle of light fades on DENISE.

A colourful computer game projects against the back wall: Rocket League, *a rocket-powered car flying through the air, hitting a gigantic football.*

ZEF. Are we playing, or what? Come on, I'm inviting you.

Lights up on ZEF (dressed in urban-ninja casuals, immaculately groomed, with the kind of hair that takes time, gel and practise to achieve), sitting across the stage from NEIL, holding a wireless gaming controller.

ZEF's computer screen is projected behind his head for the audience – playing Rocket League *in 'Free Play' mode, warming up.*

NEIL *(to ZEF)*. Shouldn't we be working?

NEIL steps into the scene – a small office, NEIL and ZEF at their respective desks.

NEIL's computer screen flickers to life, projected behind him – a 'bloop' sound as an alert pops up: 'Party invitation from CASANOVA_BOMB_3000'.

ZEF. Can't.

NEIL. We could, technically.

ZEF. You saw Mike's email. As of this morning, we work exclusively on the MOD leak. And we're forbidden from starting work until we've received our initial briefing. Have you received your initial briefing?

NEIL. No…

ZEF. Neither have I. So we can stare at the wall for an hour, or…

NEIL *picks up a wireless controller of his own. Taps a button and joins the game.*

Yes, mate! Prepare to get scored on.

The game counts down to kick-off – NEIL *vs* ZEF, *one-on-one. Their cars race towards the ball, collide and... the ball ricochets off a wall, straight into* ZEF*'s net. 'NEIL_B4_ME scored!' displays on the screen.*

What the –

NEIL. If you don't flip, you get dunked on.

ZEF. Jammy bastard. Don't even *pretend* you did that on purpose.

They kick off again – ZEF *doing better this time. The game begins in earnest,* NEIL *and* ZEF *mashing their controller buttons through what follows.*

... HANNAH (*smartly dressed, hard-edged, in a hurry*) *strides into the room behind them, a slim laptop slung under one arm. She takes in the room –*

Glaring first at NEIL, *then at* ZEF –

HANNAH (*under her breath*). Fuck's sake.

HANNAH *exits, pulling a phone out of her pocket as she leaves.* NEIL *and* ZEF *glance at each other for a moment* (*'Who was that?'*) *before resuming their game.*

A voice from the corridor – HANNAH *talking angrily into her phone.*

(*Off.*) Dom, what the fuck is this? I was promised a task force.

NEIL *and* ZEF *pause their game, panicked.*

ZEF (*quietly*). Who's that?

NEIL *shrugs.* (*'No idea.'*)

HANNAH (*off, into phone*). No, Dom. Two pyjama-clad adolescents playing video games in a cupboard does *not* constitute a bloody 'task force'.

NEIL *and* ZEF *look down at their clothes.*

ZEF (*quietly*). D'you think she knows we can hear her?

NEIL (*quietly*). I suspect she knows, but doesn't care.

HANNAH (*off*). Well, I'm starting to question Mike's judgement. There *must* be a more experienced team – (*Beat.*) No, not yet, but I'm not going to waste my time – (*Beat.*) With all due respect – is that a request, or an order? (*Beat.*) Fine.

HANNAH *re-enters the office, stony-faced. NEIL and ZEF alt-tab away from their game – both their screens showing a bland computer desktop with a corporate logo – a red ellipse orbiting a blue crown – in the centre.*

This is three-two-four-C?

ZEF. Er – yes, ma'am.

HANNAH. National Defence Info-Sec?

NEIL. Yes, ma'am.

HANNAH. Are there more of you? (*Off their confused expressions.*) Fine. Let's get this over with. I'm Hannah Barker, Deputy Director, CTD. (*Indicating a screen on the back wall.*) Does that screen work?

NEIL *and* ZEF *gawp at* HANNAH, *awestruck, as she flips open her laptop.*

ZEF. Counter-Terror?

NEIL. Mike never said anything about –

HANNAH. Turn on the screen, please, I don't have all day.

ZEF (*scrambling into action*). Yes, ma'am. Course, ma'am. The remote's… (*Shovels aside detritus on his desk.*) around here… somewhere… it's…

NEIL *grabs a TV remote from his own spotless desk – tosses it to* ZEF.

(*Catching the remote.*)… here.

ZEF *turns on the screen, offers the remote to* HANNAH. *She takes it reluctantly, as if it might harbour an infection. The screen flickers to life, displaying a PowerPoint title slide:*

'OPERATION NYX GAMMA'.

Smaller text at the top of the slide reads: 'TOP SECRET STRAP2'.

I'm Zef, this is / Neil –

HANNAH (*ignoring him*). Let me start by warning you both, in the plainest possible terms, that the information you're about to hear is –

NEIL *puts up his hand.*

How can you *possibly* have a question already?

NEIL. Have we started yet? The task force?

HANNAH. Of course you haven't started – I haven't told you what you're doing.

ZEF. We've read the briefing – Ministry of Defence has a leak. Someone's been sending stories to *The Sun* and the *Guardian*, about the state of Britain's armed forces – equipment shortages, troop morale, sexy misconduct –

NEIL. – sexual misconduct –

ZEF. – among senior officers, plus some tasty details about arms deals with Saudi Arabia. MOD wants to know who's leaking, Special Branch and BSS investigated –

NEIL. – but since they don't know one end of an ethernet cable from the other –

ZEF. – they came crawling to us for help.

HANNAH. That… is an absurd simplification of a complicated situation. As I will explain if you'll –

NEIL. So we have started, then? This is the briefing?

HANNAH. Yes, the task force has started.

NEIL *nods. He and* ZEF *start typing – their screens blasting into life, a cascade of database queries, network maps, spreadsheets, email accounts and phone logs piling up at dizzying speed.*

As I was trying to explain… The first story appeared over three years ago, under the byline of the *Guardian*'s veteran defence correspondent, Fergus Kay.

The byline photo of a grey-haired journalist appears on the projector screen.

If you turn to page two of your… (*Noticing the typing.*) For God's sake – can you not type while I'm bloody talking!

ZEF *and* NEIL *barely seem to hear her – their fingers still flying across the keyboards, their screens bouncing with new windows, coding scripts and charts.*

That's it. (*Snaps her laptop shut.*) I tried. (*Heading for the door.*) I'll be reporting your complete lack of / professionalism to –

NEIL *and* ZEF (*simultaneously*). Found her.

Pause.

ZEF *grabs the TV remote, taps a button – switching the input. A new image appears on the screen – a staff photo of a woman in her forties.*

HANNAH. Pardon?

NEIL. The leak – we found her. Her name is Alissa Clifton-Ford, she's the Senior Strategy Consultant to the Minister for Defence Procurement, before that she was –

ZEF. …Secretary to the Communications Director. We've got her red-handed for… eleven…

NEIL. …Twelve…

ZEF. …twelve of the fourteen leaked stories. Probably all of them – we'll double-check.

HANNAH. That's… ridiculous. How could you –

NEIL. Simple cross-matching algorithm. An eight-year-old child could have done it.

ZEF. Which is probably why MI5 had so much trouble.

NEIL. She leaked the first three stories by email, from an account she set up under a fake name, but then linked to her personal Hotmail account when she set it up. Schoolboy error. We've got the text messages arranging their meetings – which they didn't even encrypt. Plus the fact that Fergus Kay drafts all his articles in Microsoft Word…

ZEF.…which he then emails to himself. I swear, my dad has
better info-sec than these two.

HANNAH *peers over* ZEF's *shoulder at his screen.*

HANNAH. But – hang on, I need documentation, I need –

NEIL. We'll forward all this to your SFT.

HANNAH. Okay, but… (*Regaining her poise.*) That's twelve of
the fourteen stories – what about the other two?

NEIL. The Saudi arms deals. No comms trail on those – most
likely a different source.

HANNAH. You're saying there's a second leaker?

ZEF. Could be.

HANNAH. How long will it take you to find them?

ZEF (*trading a look with* NEIL). Maybe… couple of hours?
More if they were careful.

HANNAH. Then… I'll check back with you this afternoon.
Carry on.

ZEF *and* NEIL. Yes, ma'am.

HANNAH *starts to exit.* ZEF *calls after her –*

NEIL. One question, ma'am? Before you go.

HANNAH. What is it?

ZEF *shakes his head at* NEIL – *who ignores it.*

NEIL. It's just that… none of these leaks relate to terrorism, as
far as I can see. So why is this op running through your
office?

HANNAH. That's need-to-know.

NEIL. But –

ZEF (*cutting* NEIL *off*) .What Neil means to say is: it's a
privilege to be working with Counter-Terror – we're excited
for the opportunity, we won't let you down.

HANNAH *nods. Exits.*

Spotlight on DENISE, *upstage.*

DENISE (*to* NEIL). Okay, slow down – I need to be absolutely clear on this. Your agency hacked the communications of a British journalist, to identify their source?

NEIL. Yes.

DENISE. And was this the first time you'd done that?

NEIL. No. If a leak presented a threat to national security, the priority was to identify the source as quickly as possible. We could do that faster than Special Branch or MI5, so in urgent cases... our unit got the call.

DENISE. And you can prove this?

NEIL. I have a cache of over two hundred thousand documents, audio and video files, on three encrypted drives, which will verify every event I describe to you today.

That stops DENISE *cold.*

DENISE. Two hundred...

NEIL. Two hundred thousand. Indexed by department and subject area. Most of them top secret, some Strap 1 and 2, a few Strap 3. (*Beat.*) Hello? Are you there?

DENISE. Yes, I'm here. Sorry, just... processing. (*Then.*) Okay, I need you to understand a few things, before we go any further. First of all: leaking classified documents is a crime. You could be prosecuted under the Official Secrets Act.

NEIL. I know.

DENISE. Secondly: it's a crime for me to receive those documents. We could both end up in prison.

NEIL. I know.

DENISE. I'm not saying that's a dealbreaker, I'm just saying we need to tread very, very carefully here. There'll be a lot of lawyers, extreme scrutiny of every detail, every allegation... Because this could be big, Neil. Extremely big. The security services striking at the heart of a free press...

NEIL. Oh, no. That's not… I mean, by all means write that story too, if you think it's important. But that's not the story I'm telling. I was just setting the scene.

DENISE. 'Setting the scene'…?

NEIL. I only mentioned it because it happened on the same day as… I mean… this was the first day I ever heard the name…

ZEF (*to* NEIL). Cora who?

NEIL (*to* ZEF). Cora Preece.

The spotlight fades on DENISE, *as* NEIL *re-enters the scene with* ZEF.

ZEF. Who's Cora Priest?

NEIL. Preece. Junior staff writer at the *Guardian*. Co-wrote those last two articles, with Fergus Kay. Maybe she's got a source, leaking the Saudi stuff?

A new picture appears on the screen – the staff photo of a young female journalist, CORA, *smiling at the camera.*

ZEF. Fuck me, mate, she is… *hot* off the press. I mean… 'stop the press', because this girl is… Those must be some hot presses, because she…

NEIL. You think she's hot, I got it.

ZEF. I don't 'think' anything – she is empirically, verifiably, scientifically hot.

NEIL. Have you read the articles?

ZEF. I… skimmed 'em.

NEIL. So you know what they're about.

ZEF. Kate Middleton in a tight dress?

NEIL *rolls his eyes. Throws the articles/photos up onto the big screen from his computer. Images of Prince Charles, Prince William and Duchess Kate attending a formal gathering in Saudi Arabia.*

NEIL. Arms sales to the Saudis. Our Royal Family flies out to Riyadh twice a year, to flog British weapons to the sheiks.

ZEF. I would totally buy guns from Duchess Kate. Whatever she's selling, I'm buying.

NEIL *throws new images up onto the screen – Yemeni child soldiers brandishing rifles, under the headline: 'Child Soldiers, British Guns'.*

NEIL. Trouble is, the Saudis gave those guns to their militia in Yemen – some of them child soldiers, twelve, thirteen years old. Major scandal.

ZEF. Yikes. No wonder they've brought us in. (*Indicating his screen.*) But there's nothing about Saudi arms deals in Fergus Kay's comms, *or* Clifton-Ford's. It's like he didn't write these articles at all.

NEIL. Which leaves the only other journalist with a byline on these stories – Cora Preece.

HANNAH *enters, looking up at the picture of* CORA *projected on the wall.*

HANNAH (*indicating the photo*). You think she's the one who landed the Saudi leaks?

NEIL. Yes.

ZEF. No. (*To* NEIL.) Look, no offence, mate – I mean, I'm sure you're dying to go through her hard drive –

HANNAH. I'm going to warn you both exactly once about inappropriate behaviour –

ZEF. – but there's absolutely no way Cora Preece has a high-level Saudi intelligence source. Three years at the *Guardian*, all she's got to show for it is a bunch of blog posts about bullshit. Look at this stuff –

Articles appear on ZEF's *screen – all relating to culture and technology,*

HANNAH (*reading the headlines*). 'The Truth About Twitter Trolls'… 'Instagramorexia', 'Technology and Loneliness'…

ZEF. – also the title of Neil's autobiography.

NEIL. Thanks, mate.

ZEF. Point is, Cora Preece isn't a serious journalist. No way did she land these stories. More likely, she checked Fergus Kay's punctuation, and they gave her a byline out of pity.

NEIL. Or – she landed the stories, and they gave Fergus Kay a byline to lend them gravitas.

HANNAH. Alright, I've heard enough. Two theories, two of you, we follow up both. Zef, you go back over Fergus Kay's comms, see if you missed something. Neil, you take Cora Preece. Quickly, please – Mike wants you both back on general ops by tomorrow.

NEIL *and* ZEF. Yes, ma'am.

HANNAH *exits*.

ZEF. You owe me one, man. I'm going through a seventy-year-old man's all-caps emails to his chiropractor, while you're neck-deep in Cora Preece's hot bikini selfies. Just promise you'll share the good ones – for the old spank bank.

NEIL. I don't have a spank bank.

ZEF. Fuck off, mate – everyone's got a spank bank. After seven years in this place, I bet yours needs an encrypted hard drive all to itself…

NEIL. I don't have a spank bank.

ZEF. Well, I do, and it's very much open for business if Ms Preece is donating material. Oh, and if it turns out I'm right, you're buying the first round tonight.

NEIL. How about: last one to find the leak buys drinks all night?

ZEF. Oh, you're on.

ZEF pulls on a pair of headphones, and he and NEIL *get to work, fingers flying across their keyboards, their screens filling up with database queries, Python code, spreadsheets and network maps.*

The lights fade on ZEF, *spotlight on* NEIL, *as he addresses the audience directly.*

NEIL. Over the course of the next seven hours, I learned the following things about Cora Preece: youngest of two children, brother emigrated to Germany, mother deceased, father lives two hundred miles away, in Davenbury. Cora lives alone in a studio apartment near Royal Oak, rent is nine hundred and thirty pounds a month, bills not included. Her income from the *Guardian* is one thousand eight hundred and eighteen pounds a month, which doesn't cover her monthly outgoings. Her largest non-rent expenses are groceries and takeaway food – her favourite restaurants are Vivaldi Pizza and Dominique's Café. Her most-played artists on Spotify are Troye Sivan, The Japanese House and someone called... 'Jai Paul'. She uses her father's Netflix account, her three favourite shows are *Quarantine*, *Lost Kingdom* and *Infinity Crash*. (*To himself.*) Good show. (*Then.*) She appears to have a celebrity crush on *Saturday Night Live*'s Pete Davidson, checking his Instagram several times a day. Her boyfriend's name is Robert MacLeavy, twenty-five years old, junior account executive at DLP Communications, they've been dating for approximately six months, but judging by their comms, the relationship is... rocky. She has two repeat prescriptions, one for adapalene cream to treat mild facial acne, the other for the antibiotic trimethoprim, to treat recurring cystitis. Her latest cervical smear test showed abnormal cells, but a colposcopy gave her the all-clear. She views online pornography slightly more than once a week, on average, her preferred videos featuring oral sex, threesomes and teachers-slash-professors, alone or in combination. She's travelled extensively, though never to Saudi Arabia. But she has... (*Looks back at his screen.*) interesting...

NEIL *focuses on his computer screen, pulls on a heavy pair of headphones, and starts typing furiously. His screen* (*like* ZEF's) *piling up with new windows, new searches, new code.*

HANNAH *enters behind them, wearing a fresh suit.*

HANNAH. Christ, it smells rancid in here.

They ignore her, headphones still in place. Louder –

Guys? Where are you with the Saudi leak?

ZEF (*still typing furiously*). Coming.

HANNAH. Did either of you go home last night?

NEIL *and* ZEF (*still typing furiously*). It's coming.

ZEF. Fuck's sake, we must have… missed… something…

NEIL. Wait for it… wait for it…

> NEIL *yanks off his headphones, and throws his arms in the air.*

Got her.

ZEF (*removing his headphones*). Oh, sod off…

NEIL. I've found the leak on the Saudi stories.

> *A new face is projected on the back wall, alongside* CORA*'s. This time it's a glamorous-looking Saudi woman, wearing a loose-fitting veil.*

Ladies and gentlemen, I give you Princess Ameera Al-Mansur, of Saudi Arabia. Ex-wife of the billionaire Prince – (*Stumbling over the name.*) Khaled bin Talal Al-Saud. Now divorced, living in exile in London, where she's become increasingly close friends with… drum roll please…

ZEF (*wearily*). Cora cocking Preece.

NEIL. Cora Preece.

HANNAH. How do you know this… 'Al-Mansur' is the leak?

NEIL. Her ex-husband's on the Saudi National Security Council. She was present at the Royal Family visits mentioned in the articles.

HANNAH. Circumstantial.

NEIL. And… Cora called her last week – we still had it in the buffer. Check this out.

> NEIL *hits 'play' on an audio file on his desktop.* ZEF *and* HANNAH *listen.*

> *Lights up on* CORA (*funky clothes*) *pushing a button on her mobile phone, stage right. In her other hand,* CORA *is holding a brand-new laptop.*

A phone rings. Across the stage, lights up on AMEERA
(*wearing flowing designer clothes*), *picking up a landline
telephone.*

AMEERA (*lightly accented English*). Hello?

CORA. Ameera? Hi, it's me, Cora.

AMEERA. Cora-Cora! My darling girl – I hope this call is to
arrange your next visit for tea? I need grown-up
conversation, from someone who isn't 'staff'.

CORA. I'd love to see you, Ameera. Very soon. But first I need
to... I just received... your present.

AMEERA. Ah – it arrived! I saw your computer when you
came for lunch. Clicking old laptop, always with the egg
timer, waiting, waiting. Not good enough for a great
journalist like yourself. Great artist needs great tools.

CORA. Ameera, I'm so, so grateful to you – I cried when
I opened it. But... I'm afraid... I can't accept it.

AMEERA. Of course you can. Already accepted.

CORA. My newspaper has a strict ethics code, we're forbidden
from accepting gifts. To preserve our integrity.

A beat.

AMEERA. The stories I gave you – were they not good stories?

CORA. They were amazing, Ameera, they really... really
changed things for me, here in the office. I can't ever thank
you enough –

AMEERA. Then you take the laptop.

CORA. I just can't, I'm so sorry. Either I give this back to you,
or I'm going to have to give it to charity. It's policy.

AMEERA. Okay, I tell you what. You come here for tea, bring
the laptop. Maybe I have other stories for you. Bigger. But
you tell your bosses, you only get these stories *if...* you keep
the laptop.

CORA. I would... love to meet up again. When suits you?

AMEERA. I'm going to Paris tomorrow, back on Wednesday. Shall we say Wednesday afternoon?

NEIL *hits 'pause' on the audio file. Lights down on* CORA *and* AMEERA.

ZEF (*to* NEIL, *reluctantly*). Alright, mate, you win – what you drinking?

HANNAH (*to* ZEF). It's 11 a.m., nobody's drinking. (*To* NEIL.) You said this woman's husband was on the Saudi National Security Council?

NEIL. Ex-husband.

HANNAH. And this phone call was six days ago. So they'll be meeting up for tea…

NEIL. Tomorrow afternoon.

HANNAH. Send all this material through to me, with a one-pager – I'll run it upstairs.

NEIL. Done. It's in your SFT.

HANNAH. Excellent work, Neil.

NEIL. Team effort, ma'am.

HANNAH. Excellent work, both of you. Why don't you guys take the rest of the day, catch up on your sleep. Tomorrow you're back to your regular ops stack.

NEIL *and* ZEF (*disappointed*). What?

HANNAH. Clear?

NEIL *and* ZEF. Yes, ma'am.

HANNAH *exits.*

ZEF. Day off!

NEIL. Day off.

ZEF. Pub then cinema, or cinema then pub?

NEIL. Your choice.

ZEF. Cinema first. That way Anya can join us later, I'll get her to bring some friends. (*Teasingly.*) Maybe Liz'll come…

NEIL *throws* ZEF *a withering look.*

Come on, Liz totally has a thing for you. Or, you know, she *had* a thing for you. Before you called her stupid. But if you just apologise –

NEIL. I didn't call her stupid.

ZEF. I was there, you definitely called her

NEIL. I summarised a scientific finding –

ZEF. – that linguists are thick.

NEIL. – that on average, the measured IQs of maths and science graduates are higher than modern-language graduates, according to multiple studies –

ZEF. Mate, even if that's true –

NEIL. – Which it is –

ZEF. – you don't say that to a girl who works as a fucking *translator.*

NEIL. It's a population average! You can't get offended by averages.

ZEF. If I told you that, on average, you are useless with women, would you be offended?

NEIL. Of course not.

ZEF. Because you're a robot.

NEIL. Because the statistics back you up. (*Then.*) You know what, I actually do have plans tonight. I think I'm gonna head home.

ZEF. We just impressed the Deputy Director of Counter-cocking Terror. That calls for beer and girls and… celebration. Come on, spend some time in meatspace, interact with real human beings / for a –

NEIL. I interact with plenty of –

ZEF. Reddit doesn't count.

Beat.

NEIL. I've got reading to catch up on. A bunch of bash scripts to debug.

ZEF. 'Bash scripts', are you… [… *kidding me?'*] Alright, I give up. You have fun in your bedsit, alone. (*More gently.*) I'll… see you tomorrow, yeah?

NEIL. Have fun.

> ZEF *exits*. NEIL *grabs his bicycle helmet, and steps into –*

> *– his bedsit. A spartan, organised space: bed, desk, office chair with a small fridge. Lights down on the office.*

> NEIL *hangs up his bike helmet, sits at his desk. Fires up his computer. The screen projects against the back wall – dozens of windows tiled across the screen: code editors, plain-text bash scripts and GitHub pages.* NEIL *stares at his screen for a moment. Fidgets. Swivels in his chair, trying to decide what to do.*

> *A thought hits him. He opens up Tor Browser on his computer. A dialogue box opens:* '**Connecting to the Tor network… Establishing a Tor circuit…**' *Then –* '**Welcome to Tor Browser. You are now free to browse the Internet anonymously.**'

> *He types* '**Cora Preece Guardian**' *into the address bar. A search page loads (DuckDuckGo) – a list of Cora's articles filling the screen.* NEIL *clicks on the top link:* '**Technology and Loneliness.**' *A* Guardian *article loads, with the subheading:* '**Can we find real intimacy, in the age of social media?**'

> *Lights rise on* CORA *standing centre-stage, looking out at the audience.*

CORA. No one should be lonely, in the age of the internet. From Facebook to Twitter, Tinder to Grindr, instant connection with our fellow human beings is never more than a click, a tap or a swipe away.

> *The first line of the article is:* '**No one should be lonely, in the age of the internet**' … NEIL *scrolls down, reading quickly.*

Why, then, do so many of us still feel lonely? More lonely, according to surveys, than before the internet arrived. A recent study showed that it's no longer the elderly and isolated who feel the most lonely – it's the young and hyper-connected. Forty per cent of young Britons report that they 'always or often' feel lonely – double the rate of their Luddite grandparents. And the more time they spend on social media, the more lonely they report feeling.

NEIL *opens a new tab – calls up* CORA*'s Facebook page. It's privacy protected, but some of her photos are public – holiday snaps, selfies, family photos.*

Rates of depression and anxiety, self-harm and suicide have sky-rocketed among Britain's teenagers. We've never been more connected, but never felt more alone.

NEIL *scrolls through* CORA*'s photos, as she continues.*

It wasn't supposed to be this way. In its early days, the internet seemed to promise the Introvert's Holy Grail: the chance to have a vibrant social life, without ever leaving the house. So where did it all go wrong?

NEIL *pulls up new tabs in his browser –* CORA*'s Instagram account, her Twitter.*

It seems that the dopamine rush we get from our Retweets, Shares and Likes, leaves some deeper part of our psyche unsatisfied. Our primate brains can tell the difference between a 'Like' and being liked, between being Shared and truly sharing, between a Swipe and physical, human touch. The cure for loneliness, it turns out, isn't being 'Followed' or looked at. It's being *seen*. In all our messy, dysfunctional, infuriating glory.

NEIL *lingers on a photo of* CORA*, as –*

ZEF. Check your messages.

Lights up on ZEF*, at his computer in the office.* NEIL *stands, grabs a couple of cans of Red Bull, and enters the office. Lights down on* NEIL*'s studio.*

NEIL. What?

ZEF. Check. Your. Messages.

NEIL. New op?

ZEF. Big news. Huge. We've got the keys to the Ferrari.

NEIL. What?

> NEIL *puts one of the Red Bulls on* ZEF*'s desk, then sits at his own terminal. A secure message with the heading '**NYX GAMMA – Warrant Approval**' is waiting for him.*

ZEF. Cora Preece is meeting Al-Mansur today, Barker wants real-time surveillance of the meet, she wants *us* to do the surveilling, which means...

NEIL. You're kidding –

ZEF. We get to play with the bazookas. Full access to Counter-Terror's suite of bad-ass – and I mean *Bad. Ass.* – exploitation tools. Just look at this shit.

> NEIL *opens a directory called '**CNE**' in his terminal. He queries the contents – a list of executable files unspooling on his screen. He reads them off, bemused by the names –*

NEIL. What the hell is... 'Foggybottom'?

ZEF. Records the target's browsing history, hoovers up their passwords and login details.

NEIL. 'Grok'?

ZEF. Records every keystroke they make.

NEIL. 'Nosey Smurf'.

ZEF. Remotely access microphones on any device.

NEIL. 'Tracker Smurf'. Wait, I can guess –

ZEF. Track the target's location, using GPS and wireless triangulation. Then there's my absolute favourite...

NEIL. 'Gumfish'?

ZEF. Sweet, sweet Gumfish. Switch on the camera on any target device and snap photos to our heart's content.

NEIL. Jesus.

ZEF. Hallelujah.

NEIL. But… shouldn't BSS be handling this? It's domestic surveillance, that's literally what they're for.

ZEF. I asked. Barker says we're keeping this in-house, till we know what we're dealing with – warrants already approved. And since she's *so impressed* with our work so far, we get to lead on the op. Real-time surveillance, mate! Proper *Spooks* stuff. So come on, let's take these babies for a spin.

ZEF *starts typing rapidly – calling up Gumfish, selecting 'Target #819-658-562: Preece, C' from a drop-down menu, calling up her phone number, IMEI, known IP addresses, etc.*

Lights up on AMEERA *and* CORA, *sitting on a luxurious sofa in* AMEERA*'s house. Expensive art lines the walls, antiques and ornate rugs.*

On the coffee table in front of them is a lavish spread of sandwiches, snacks, cakes and sweets. NEIL *pulls on a pair of headphones, as he and* ZEF *listen in on the conversation.*

CORA *(mouth full)*. This is divine, Ameera…

AMEERA. You must eat, Cora-Cora, you're skin and bones. (*Offering a platter of pastries.*) Try the samboosak – my sister's favourite.

CORA *takes the proffered pastry.*

Better. You are just like her – my sister, Hala. Always running, running, never stopping to eat a proper meal. Terrible for your health.

CORA. If this is how you have 'tea', I have no idea how you manage dinner.

AMEERA. I keep begging her to come here too. Hala – to come to London, join me and little Sahar. Away from the Kingdom. Far from Khaled's reach.

CORA. You think your husban–… your ex-husband would hurt your sister?

AMEERA. If he thought it would force me home, he'd string her up in Deera Square. And if I returned, he would stone me to death on the same spot. Four years since I left him, and still he cannot accept it. Always telling your government to send me home – he pulls every string, calls every favour. I know because I read his emails.

A beat.

CORA. I'm sorry, you… read your husband's emails?

AMEERA. Of course! His password never changes. Every morning, before I feed Sahar, I read his messages. To find out what that snake has been doing, while I've been sleeping. I must stay one step of ahead of him, always.

CORA. And is that… is that why you wanted to see me? Do you want to… tell your story, in public?

AMEERA. Tsh. Who cares about me? Little princess who fell in love with an Englishman. I would not get so much sympathy, I think.

CORA. The mother of a young child, being hounded by a member of the Saudi Royal Family? Everyone would take your side. And bringing it out into the open – we could force him to stop.

AMEERA. He will never stop. His heart is a fist. Every day he lashes out, every day I dodge as best I can. But. Khaled's family has a weapon – you say 'a secret weapon', yes? And he asks his brothers, night and day, to use it against me. He berates them – 'How can you let this *woman* defy us?' And this weapon – I cannot dodge. This weapon, we must shatter. And now, Cora-Cora, you will need your notebook.

Spotlight on DENISE, *ashen-faced, as the light fades down on* AMEERA *and* CORA.

DENISE (*to* NEIL). I know what comes next.

Lights up on an editor's office at the Guardian. *Desk piled with papers, books and magazines.* CORA *standing on one side of the desk, notebook in hand.*

CORA. I want to be lead on this, Dee. It's my source, my story.

DENISE *throws a long, cold gaze at* NEIL.

DENISE (*to* NEIL). You fucking bastard.

Through what follows, NEIL *and* ZEF *are listening in.*

CORA. Promise me.

DENISE *grimaces. Then, reluctantly, she steps into the scene with* CORA, *taking a seat behind the desk. It's* DENISE*'s office –* CORA *standing across from her.*

DENISE (*sipping a coffee*). That depends on what the story is.

CORA. And I don't want to be... no offence, but I don't want to be stuck with Fergus this time. Or sent back to – again, no offence – back to Bloggers' Corner. This is my third scoop, I've done my time, I'm ready to –

DENISE. You can't haggle with me, unless you tell me what you're selling.

CORA. It's about Ameera.

DENISE. Your tame Saudi princess – the asylum seeker?

CORA. – who's already come through with two rock-solid stories. Which I now think were... auditions. Testing us, to see if we'd preserve her anonymity. Which we did. And now she's ready to drop the fucking atom bomb, Dee. And she wants to give it to us. To me. Which is why you've got to let me lead on this –

DENISE. Drop your bomb on me, and we'll see. Is this a follow-up on the arms sales?

CORA. So much bigger. Okay, Ameera, she reads her ex-husband's emails. She knows his password, he hasn't changed it. And the husband, Prince Khaled, he wants her deported – he's obsessed with it. Constantly emailing his family, begging them to pull strings with our government, to get her kicked out.

DENISE. That's hardly surprising –

CORA. And that's not the story. The strings are the story.

DENISE. Meaning?

CORA. In his emails to his brothers, Prince Khaled keeps referring to… (*Looks at her notebook.*) the 'ḵadam'. I might be pronouncing that wrong. He's always asking – 'Why can't the ḵadam deport her? Why aren't the ḵadam having her arrested?'

DENISE. And who are the… 'ha-dam'…?

CORA. The word means… 'servants'. Or 'footmen', or even 'maids'. It's not a respectful term, but it seems to be what they call them –

DENISE. What they call *whom*?

CORA. It's their pet name for the British officials… and Members of Parliament, whom they consider to be… on their payroll. Hired help. Servants. We're talking MPs, Lords, senior civil servants in multiple departments, taking bribes from the Saudi Royal Family. Massive cash transfers into untraceable off-shore accounts – millions of pounds in total. *That's* the story.

Pause. DENISE *puts down her coffee mug.*

DENISE. She gave you names?

CORA. Not yet. But she will.

DENISE. There's a list?

CORA. Better. There's a spreadsheet. Names. Payments. Dates. Bank-account numbers. All of it.

DENISE. How many names?

CORA. She didn't say – but I saw dozens, at least.

DENISE. So she showed you this spreadsheet?

CORA. It was in Arabic, but… yes, she showed me the spreadsheet.

DENISE. But you have no idea what it actually said – ?

CORA. We can hire translators –

DENISE. But we have no guarantee of authenticity –

CORA. And she knows that. Which is why she's prepared to give us every single email from his account, spanning the

full seven years since he first opened it. We cross-check
those with some of the recipients to confirm authenticity,
and –

DENISE. What's her price?

CORA. She just wants to stay in England – to stop these corrupt
officials from conspiring to have her deported.

DENISE. Enough of the soft-sell. Did she say a number, or are
we supposed to – ?

CORA. Two hundred thousand pounds. (*Pause.*) Her legal fees,
fighting her husband, are quite substantial. (*Pause.*) I know
it's a lot of money, but for the scoop of the decade –

DENISE. You believe her?

CORA. She's never lied to me. Her last two stories checked out,
every detail. She's solid, Dee.

Pause. DENISE *seems deep in thought.*

So...?

DENISE. I need to make some phone calls. Go back to your
desk, don't leave the office. Have you told anyone else about
this, at all?

CORA. Of course not.

DENISE. Good. Then... give me some time. If this is real, we'll
need a whole team on it.

CORA. And I'll lead that team?

DENISE. Cora –

CORA. What? This is my story –

DENISE. There's a way we do these things, Cora. We'll need to
bring in Ewan, Mina, Paul, and Fergus –

CORA. Dee –

DENISE (*insistent*). – *and Fergus*. And to be brutally honest –
no, you won't be leading that team. This is absolutely not the
right place for you to start –

CORA. But –

DENISE. – but nothing, this calls for experienced hacks, who know the smell of bullshit from decades of wading through it –

CORA. This is exactly what I'm talking about! This fucking gerontocracy – it's not a story unless some grey-haired man gives the nod. I should just take this to bloody WikiLeaks –

DENISE. Listen to me, Cora – really listen. A story like this can make careers – but it can also break them. More than that, it can ruin the lives of journalists, sources, editors, owners. Nobody's going to print a word without bullet-proof – I mean *bullet-proof* – verification. Which you have not yet delivered. Now sit at your desk, while I call –

CORA. *Fuck's* sake…

> CORA *begins storming towards the exit.* DENISE *calls her back –*

DENISE. Cora. You don't need to worry about… 'Bloggers' Corner'. If this is what you say it is, your life is going to change. A lot of lives are going to change. Okay?

> CORA *hesitates a moment… then nods, sullenly.*

Excellent work. Truly.

> CORA *manages a half-smile, and exits. As the lights fade on* DENISE, *they rise on* NEIL *and* ZEF, *sitting at their computer screens, headphones in place. Slowly, they remove their headphones and turn to look at each other.*

ZEF. Fuck me.

NEIL. Yeah.

ZEF. I mean, this is…

NEIL. Yeah.

> HANNAH *sweeps into their office –*

HANNAH. As of now we're escalating to round-the-clock surveillance, real-time monitoring of Cora Preece and Ameera Al-Mansur. You'll be working in shifts with a team from my office. Any questions?

ZEF *raises his hand*.

ZEF. Shouldn't BSS be taking over?

HANNAH. They're looped in, but for now this stays with us. Anything else?

NEIL. Yeah... what does any of this have to do with terrorism? There's been no mention of –

HANNAH (*impatient*). Any *sensible* questions? (*Beat.*) Okay, then. Who's on Al-Mansur, who's on Preece?

The boys look at each other.

ZEF. RPS? Winner gets Preece.

HANNAH. What's RPS?

NEIL. It's an algorithm we use, to allocate responsibilities.

NEIL *turns to* ZEF, *each of them holding up a fist.*

NEIL *and* ZEF. One, two, three –

They're playing Rock, Paper, Scissors. NEIL goes for Rock, ZEF goes for Scissors.

ZEF. Fuck it!

NEIL. Every time.

HANNAH *smiles*.

HANNAH. That's settled, then. Keep up the good work.

HANNAH *exits*.

ZEF. I'll give you... my Maltesers, if you let me take Preece.

NEIL (*pulling on his headphones*). The gods of RPS have spoken.

ZEF. Maltesers and a Red Bull. Two Red Bulls.

NEIL *doesn't reply.*

Dammit. Fine. If you need me, I'll be machine-translating Arabic text messages about nappies and nursery schools.

ZEF *pulls on his headphones*. NEIL *does the same*.

Lights up on CORA*'s apartment. A tiny London studio flat –
sofa and TV, cramped kitchenette, cheap bed crammed into
one corner.*

CORA *and* ROB, *her boyfriend, are on the sofa drinking
cheap sparkling wine.* NEIL *listens on headphones as they
talk to each other –*

ROB.…it's fine, I get it. You just said you'd come, that's all.
I told everyone.

CORA. Babe, I'm sorry – but this is a huge story. Like, 'once in
a career' huge. I've got to work.

ROB. But you can't tell me what the story is.

CORA. Not yet, no. It's a 'secret squirrel' thing, we're not
meant to talk about it.

ROB. Okay, okay. I'll tell them you're busy. (*Then.*) You know…
if you don't want to come, you can just say so. You don't have
to, like, make something up.

CORA. What does *that* mean?

ROB. It means… just be honest with me. You don't really like
Rambo, you don't want to go to his party, so just say that.

CORA. Okay, first of all – can we call your friends by their real
names, not their rugby-lad whatevers?

ROB. It's what we call each other, it's affectionate.

CORA. And secondly, where do you get off, telling me I'm
'lying' about having to work?

ZEF*'s taken off his headphones, packing up to go home.
The lights dim for a moment on* ROB *and* CORA, *as –*

ZEF (*to* NEIL). Mate – you done for the day? Pint?

NEIL. Er… no, I've got a bit more to do here. Could be
important.

ZEF. Seriously? I thought you handed over to the night shift.

NEIL. I did, but… they're having connection problems – packet
loss. I'm staying on while they iron it out.

ZEF. Amateurs. Don't let 'em keep you here all night, okay?

NEIL. I won't.

ZEF *exits. Lights up on* ROB *and* CORA, *now deep into an argument –* CORA *pouring herself a generous measure of vodka, topping it up with orange juice.*

CORA. So my work's a joke to you, is what you're saying. I couldn't *possibly* be doing something more important than... attending Bing-Bong and Dildo's barbecue?

ROB. It's Bang-Bang and Tilly, and it's their *engagement party.* (*Re: her drink.*) How much vodka are you putting in there?

CORA. Exactly the right amount.

ROB. Two bottles of wine not enough for you?

CORA (*overlapping*). You drank those too –

ROB (*overlapping, louder*). A glass, I had one glass.

CORA. I'll stop drinking when you stop shouting.

ROB. I'm not shouting! I'm asking you, politely, to make some time to see my friends – it's important to me.

CORA. And my work is important to me.

ROB. – You're a blogger, not bloody... Veronica Mars.

CORA. I am not a fucking blogger.

ROB. Who can forget such classics as: 'Twelve Facts About Sharks You Won't Believe', or, or 'Tinder Horror Stories That'll Scar You For Life'.

CORA (*overlapping*). Sure, sure, belittle my work, that's great, Rob, very grown up –

ROB. 'How To Lose Friends and Drink Too Much'? I bet your editor'll love that one.

CORA. Get the fuck out. Get the fuck out of my flat, right now.

ROB. I'm gone, I'm gone. Enjoy drinking alone – for the rest of your sad, lonely life.

ROB *exits, slamming the door – the sound startling* NEIL.

CORA. Fuck.

NEIL (*under his breath*). Dickhead.

CORA *grabs her phone, unlocks it (her screen mirrored on* NEIL*'s laptop). Opens up her contacts. Hovers her finger over 'DAD'. But… decides against calling. Switches off her phone again.*

She opens her laptop, and an alert appears on NEIL*'s screen – '**Target #819-658-562: device online.**' He opens a new window, mirroring* CORA*'s laptop.* NEIL *taps in a command, and another window appears –* CORA*'s face, as seen through her laptop's camera.*

CORA *opens up Netflix. Scrolls through the recommended shows. Hovers her mouse over a couple of romantic comedies. Changes her mind. She clicks on* Infinity Crash *instead – a thumbnail image of a tiny spaceship in a vast expanse of stars. Hovers her mouse over the latest episode – '**Season 3, Episode 1.**'*

(*Shaking his head.*) You haven't finished season two yet.

CORA *realises the same thing. Clicks on '**Season 2.**' Selects an unwatched episode. As it starts playing,* NEIL *opens his desk drawer, grabs a tube of Pringles.*

CORA *pours herself another drink, wraps herself up in a blanket.* NEIL *resizes the window showing her laptop screen – making it bigger. Opens his crisps, leans back in his chair. Starts watching the show with her.*

The lights fade down on CORA*, the Netflix show fading to black.* NEIL *slumps in his chair, eyes closed – asleep.*

The lights on NEIL *brighten – the start of a new day.*

ZEF *enters the office, wearing different clothes. Sees* NEIL *asleep at his desk – and urgently taps him awake –*

ZEF. Mate. Wake up.

NEIL (*groggy*). Hm…?

HANNAH *enters.*

HANNAH. Morning, boys.

NEIL *and* ZEF. Morning, boss. / Morning, ma'am.

HANNAH. Good news from on high. You were top of the agenda at Senior Staff this morning – this op's gone all the way to Fred's desk.

ZEF (*awestruck*). Seriously, the Director –?

HANNAH. – is officially 'extremely impressed' with this unit's work. Well done, guys, really. Big win. But, now that BSS are on board, you get to take a break. Tie off whatever you're working on, index it, annotate it, and drop it in the shared drive. Then take the rest of the day off. Go grab a drink or five. Or better yet – get some sleep.

ZEF. We don't need a break, boss. Can of Red Bull and a Snickers, we're good to go.

HANNAH. It wasn't a suggestion. You're both to go dark on Cora Preece and Al-Mansur, effective immediately.

NEIL. What…?

HANNAH. As of now, you're back to general ops. Mike's got a backlog the size of this building.

ZEF. But… this is the big day. They're meeting tonight – why are we off the op?

HANNAH. That's need-to-know.

NEIL. Who's taking over from us?

HANNAH. Also need-to-know.

ZEF. Those BSS bastards, jumping in to steal the credit –

HANNAH. Guys, I'm as unhappy about this as you are, but we have orders, we're going to follow them. Index, flag and bag, then back to your info-sec work.

HANNAH *exits.* NEIL *and* ZEF *look at each other in disbelief.*

ZEF. What the actual fuck?

The lights change – the end of the day. NEIL *and* ZEF *grab their bags and bike helmets, and head out of the office. But…*

… NEIL doesn't leave. He hovers in the doorway. Checks the corridor. Then turns back to his desk.

NEIL (*to the audience*). The thing is, I *could* check on her. I mean, it's technically possible. Fire up the surveillance tools, scrub the logs when I'm done.

He turns on his computer – the screen projecting behind him. He hesitates. Checks behind him again. Then pulls up the 'CNE' folder. Arrows down to the Nosey Smurf tool. He pauses. Then launches it.

NEIL *clicks the* **'Target'** *menu. A list of targets spools down. He pauses again. His cursor hovers over* **'Target #819-658-562: Preece, C.'**

Spotlight on DENISE.

DENISE. You didn't.

NEIL. I wouldn't be the first. To use our surveillance tools for… personal reasons. We hear rumours, disciplinary procedures – people who checked on their wives, husbands, exes, crushes. It's common enough that we have a word for it: 'LOVEINT'. Collecting intelligence from people you lo–

He stops himself. A pause. He closes the Nosey Smurf window with a keystroke.

It wasn't worth the risk.

NEIL *shuts off his computer. Walks out of the office.*

Lights up on NEIL*'s bedroom –* NEIL *walking quickly inside.*

I went home, played *World of Warcraft* till 4 a.m., took three Nytol… and overslept. But when I staggered in the next morning –

ZEF (*off*). Mate – have you seen the news?

ZEF *charges into the office, pulling off his coat – the start of a new day.* NEIL *enters behind him.*

NEIL. Something from Barker?

ZEF. No, I mean the actual news. BBC. (*Off* NEIL*'s blank look.*) She's dead. She's fucking dead.

A beat. NEIL *reacts with horror –*

NEIL. No. *No*. Cora...?

ZEF. Not her – the princess, Ameera, she died last night. Look –

ZEF *elbows* NEIL *aside, calls up various news websites – projected against the back wall. Headlines pop up:* **'Tragic End for Asylum-Seeking Saudi Princess'**... **'Death of a Princess'**...

NEIL *grabs the keyboard from* ZEF, *clicks on a story – revealing a smiling picture of* AMEERA, *heading an article about her 'tragic fall' from a balcony.*

ZEF. Third-storey balcony. Police won't say if she fell, jumped or got pushed.

NEIL. Fuck... (*Scrolls down, past photos of* AMEERA, *of her Kensington home.*) What about Cora? Is she okay?

ZEF. Doubt it. (*Off* NEIL*'s horrified look.*) No, she's not hurt, it's just... she's the one who found Ameera. Lying on the front lawn, bleeding to death. *Guardian* says she died in Cora's arms.

NEIL *clicks through to the* Guardian *website, finds the headline:* **'Saudi Princess Falls to Her Death in Kensington'**. *Clicks on it, scans the article – this one with a staff photo of* CORA, *alongside images of* AMEERA.

NEIL. Jesus.

ZEF. Yeah.

NEIL. Have we... is there any... message from Barker?

ZEF. Nothing. She's not answering her phone.

NEIL. Anything on GCWiki?

ZEF. Not a word. We're civilians on this, mate – reading the news like every other twat. Fucking BSS – we hand over the op, they blow it to shit in less than a day.

NEIL. You think MI5 did this?

ZEF. I think they're incompetent. If we'd kept this in-house, she'd still be alive. (*Then.*) She had a kid, man. A three-year-old fucking kid.

NEIL *can see* ZEF's *upset, but isn't sure what to say. After a moment –*

NEIL. Should… we be back up on their phones? Maybe figure out what happened. The warrants are still active, so –

ZEF. Can't. Not without the nod from Barker. (*Standing.*) Fuck it, I'm gonna find her.

NEIL. She's a Deputy Director, you can't just barge in –

ZEF. Watch me.

ZEF *charges out of the office.* NEIL *watches him go. Waits a moment. Then fires up the Nosey Smurf surveillance tool on his computer. No hesitation this time – he clicks on* **'TARGET #819-658-562. IMEI: 8143213548192'**, *and pulls on his headphones.*

CORA. This is bullshit, Dee, fucking BULLSHIT.

Lights up on DENISE's *desk at the* Guardian – CORA *wearing ill-fitting clothes, pacing the room, extremely agitated, clutching a copy of the newspaper in one hand, her mobile phone in the other.* DENISE *is calm, leaning back against her desk –*

DENISE. Cora, sit down, please. Have some tea or –

CORA. Fuck sitting, I've been sitting for hours. Police made me sit, Ewan made me sit – we all sat down and then *nobody fucking listened to me.*

DENISE. I'm sure they were listening very closely –

CORA (*waving the newspaper*). Then how is *this*… this… horseshit our coverage? 'SAUDI PRINCESS FALLS TO HER DEATH'. 'Falls'! Did she trip on the fucking pavement?

DENISE. Please, Cora –

CORA. 'Murdered' – how hard is it to use that word? It's only eight letters, you could bump up the font. 'SAUDI PRINCESS MURDERED'…

DENISE. You know we can't write 'murdered' without proof –

CORA. Oh, if only there was some sort of proof like, I don't know, a woman bleeding to death on her fucking lawn? Ewan is just *useless* – he doesn't mention the spreadsheet, the bribes, the emails –

DENISE. We never saw the spreadsheet, Cora.

CORA. I saw it!

DENISE. You saw a spreadsheet with Arabic text –

CORA. So Ameera's a liar, now, is she? And I'm a liar too? Perhaps you should THROW ME OUT THE FUCKING WINDOW AS WELL?

Pause. CORA *shaking with adrenaline,* DENISE *still calm – but clearly concerned.*

Sorry... I'm sorry, it's not your fault...

DENISE. Have you been home yet? Have you slept?

CORA (*ignoring the question*). The police aren't even looking for the killer – their questions were just bovine.

DENISE. Is that... (*Hesitates.*) On your neck. (*Indicates a smudge of dried blood on* CORA*'s throat.*) Have you showered?

CORA. They kept asking about Ameera's mental health – Ameera's!

DENISE. At least... hang on... (*Rummages in her handbag.*) Here –

DENISE *holds out a packet of wet wipes.* CORA *takes one, wipes her neck.*

CORA. As if it matters what mood she was in, when she was *shoved off the third floor* like a bag of... a bag of...

CORA *looks down at the dark-red smear on the wet wipe. She starts to cry.*

DENISE. Hey. Hey...

DENISE *hugs* CORA, *who rocks with sobs.*

CORA (*between sobs*). She was... looking at me when she...

DENISE. I know.

CORA. We didn't protect her…

DENISE. Sssssh.

CORA (*quietly*). I didn't protect her…

> DENISE *holds* CORA. *Looks across towards* NEIL, *accusingly.*

DENISE (*to* NEIL). You heard all that, I suppose?

> NEIL *says nothing.*

Hell of a job you've got.

> NEIL *meets* DENISE*'s gaze for a moment. Before –*

HANNAH (*off*). Don't barrack me, Zef – I'm not discussing this in a bloody corridor.

> NEIL *yanks off his headphones, shuts down the surveillance tool, as* HANNAH *enters with* ZEF. *Lights down on* DENISE *and* CORA.

ZEF (*to* HANNAH). But the timing's insane. We're ordered to 'go dark' on a target, and within six hours, she's dead on her own front lawn?

HANNAH. Look, I know you have questions – we all do. I've been on the phone for four hours, but right now I know as much as you do. Everyone's scrambling on this, BSS, us, the Met, nobody knows what happened.

NEIL. Was she murdered?

HANNAH. Police say 'no sign of a struggle', they're waiting on autopsy results. That's all we know.

ZEF. What about BSS? They were meant to be watching her – so what did they fucking see?

HANNAH. They had a van outside, didn't see anything suspicious. At least, that's what they're telling us.

NEIL. Then shouldn't we be back up on this? We've still got access to Cora's phone –

HANNAH. Absolutely not. Last thing we need is a dozen different agencies charging in, tripping over each other.

We've played our role, if we're asked to do more, then we will – you'll be the first to know.

ZEF. What about that spreadsheet? The CNE guys were hacking Ameera's laptop, just before we went dark. Did we get a copy – ?

HANNAH. I don't know.

NEIL. You don't know, or you can't tell us?

HANNAH. I mean, 'I don't know'. Guys. If Al-Mansur's claims are true – if she really had a list of British officials in the pay of the Saudis – that would be… beyond incendiary. Thermonuclear. If anyone in this building has that file, they're not going to be broadcasting the fact. So if you respect my intelligence even slightly – don't ask me again. (*Then.*) I'm sorry the op ended this way. It's a contact sport, sometimes… it's messy. But you two did excellent work. Time to move on.

NEIL *and* ZEF. Yes, ma'am.

HANNAH *exits.*

NEIL. So that's it? No one's going to tell us anything?

ZEF. Cogs in a machine, mate.

NEIL. Cogs in a machine.

NEIL *and* ZEF *return to work, as the lights fade on the office.*

Lights up on NEIL*'s bedroom.* NEIL *grabs his bag and bike helmet, leaves the office, entering his bedroom. Drops his clobber and sits on his bed.*

He grabs his laptop. Fires it up – his screen projected against the back wall. Opens up his SSH client. Tunnels into his office workstation. Fires up Gumfish.

A new window pops open on NEIL*'s screen: streaming video from a low-quality camera – seemingly pointing at a dimly-lit wall.* NEIL *squints at his laptop. Shadows are playing across the 'wall' on the screen, but it's impossible to make out what's happening. A high-pitched sound through the* *laptop speakers – a strangled half-sob.* NEIL *tilts his head, trying to work out what he's looking at.*

Lights up on CORA*'s apartment.* CORA*'s curled up on her bed, crying softly. Restlessly shifting around, as if in constant pain, trying to find a position where it doesn't hurt. She reaches for her phone on the nightstand. As she does so –*

Her face appears on NEIL*'s laptop. Filling the frame – tear-streaked, sleep-deprived. He's looking through her phone's camera. A new window pops up on his screen, this one mirroring the touchscreen of* CORA*'s phone as –*

CORA *taps into her messages – a conversation with 'DEE'. Taps out a message. '**Anything new???**' She sends the message, then reaches for a half-drunk glass of wine on the nightstand. Takes a gulp.*

*Her phone chirrups – a new message. '**DEE: I'll call you if anything breaks. Is your dad there with you?**'*

CORA. Fuck's sake.

CORA *taps out a reply: '**He's here. Looking after me.**'*

NEIL (*under his breath*). No he isn't.

A quick reply on CORA*'s screen: '**DEE: I'm glad. Try to get some sleep, we'll speak first thing.**'*

CORA. Useless. Useless, USELESS fucking…

The video footage on NEIL*'s screen spins wildly as –*

– CORA *tosses her phone onto the floor. Turns off the light. Curls up on the bed.* NEIL *can only see a black rectangle –* CORA*'s unlit ceiling – through the phone's camera. But he can hear her low keening, interspersed with violent sobs.*

NEIL *flexes his hands over his keyboard. Impotent, frustrated. He moves his cursor to shut down the window… but changes his mind. Leaves it open. Turns off the lights. Lies down on his side, lit only by the glow from his laptop screen. Listens to* CORA *crying.*

As the light slowly fades on CORA *–*

Spotlight on DENISE.

DENISE. You were ordered to stop surveilling Cora.

NEIL. Yes.

DENISE. But you didn't.

NEIL. No.

DENISE. Why?

NEIL. Technically... the warrants were still active. We'd already hacked the screen-monitoring software, I could edit the activity logs –

DENISE. No, that's *how* you did it. I'm asking why.

NEIL *seems uncomfortable. Considers his answer.*

NEIL. Because I could.

CORA. Gone, all of them. Vanished.

Lights up on CORA *in* DENISE*'s office, notepad in hand, looking pale and sleep-deprived – but also wired, slightly manic.* DENISE *steps into the scene – eyeing* CORA *with concern.*

NEIL *pulls on his headphones, listening.*

The police didn't find a single electronic device in Ameera's home – no laptops, no tablets, even her fucking TiVo was gone.

DENISE. You know this how?

CORA. The DCI's a soft touch, let a few things slip in my second interview. I know for a fact Ameera had a laptop, an iMac, two iPhones – I saw them myself. If she took her own life – as they *keep* fucking implying – are we supposed to believe she took all her computers to Oxfam first?

DENISE. Any way to trace them?

CORA. Mina says 'no', not without her passwords. But whoever took them, they must have known about the spreadsheet. The deal we were making. Ameera was killed *an hour* before we were due to meet. That's not coincidence, that's panic.

Somebody's hand being forced. The question is – how did they know?

DENISE. Are you asking rhetorically, or –?

CORA. Surveillance. It's the only way. Somebody was watching, somebody was listening. Maybe to us, maybe to Ameera, maybe both.

NEIL *brings his hands to his headphones… then brings them down again.*

We need to get our phones checked for spyware – you, me, Paul, Mina and Fergus. For all we know, they're listening right now.

DENISE *glares at* NEIL *for a moment. Then –*

DENISE. I doubt that, Cora. But, by all means check our phones.

CORA. Great. (*Grabs* DENISE*'s mobile phone off the desk.*) I can have it back by this evening, Mina knows a place –

DENISE. Whoa, whoa – not right this second, I'm expecting a call.

CORA (*impatient*). When will it finish?

DENISE. Cora, slow down, you're being a little… (*Then.*) Have you been drinking?

CORA. No. *No.* (*Then.*) I had some wine with lunch, who gives a shit? (*Quickly, aggressively.*) When you've finished your call, and you've got time to take this seriously – give Mina your phone, okay?

CORA *exits, leaving an uneasy* DENISE *in her wake.*

ZEF. Up, up, down, down, left, right, left, right, A, B, Start.

Lights up on ZEF, *in* NEIL*'s bedroom, cross-legged on the bed – a game controller in his hand.*

NEIL. I thought we said 'no cheat codes'.

ZEF. Yeah, well, I've changed my mind – but it's not bloody working.

NEIL. It works fine.

NEIL *steps out of the office, joins* ZEF *in his bedsit – as tinny eight-bit music plays, a retro Nintendo game –* Gradius *– projected behind them.* NEIL *and* ZEF *are playing two-player co-op mode, each controlling a tiny spaceship, battling alien vessels.*

ZEF. It's this shitty emulator, mate – doesn't support the Contra code. (*Tapping the controller.*) Up, up, down, down, left, right, left, right, A, B, Start. (*Unpauses the game.*) See? I should have thirty lives and all the power-ups. I've got fuck-bugger-all.

NEIL. Because you're getting the code wrong.

ZEF (*outraged*). How *dare* you. I grew up on cheat codes, mate. *Doom, Quake, GoldenEye –* I am the god of god modes.

NEIL. Is that so. Let me try. (*Pauses the game. Taps rapidly on his controller. A blooping tone sounds.* NEIL *unpauses the game – now with thirty lives, and a massively souped-up spaceship.*) Ta-dah. God mode.

NEIL*'s spaceship zips around the screen, laying waste to the alien ships.*

ZEF. You total bastard – what did you do?

NEIL. Uh-uh. If you don't know the code, you don't get the mode.

ZEF. Come on – I'm your wingman. Help me out –

NEIL. Only if you say 'Neil is the god of god modes.'

Beat. ZEF *is reluctant, but...*

ZEF (*grudgingly*). Neilsthegodofgodmodes.

NEIL. Didn't hear you.

ZEF. Neil's the god of god modes – okay? What's the code?

NEIL. It's B then A – you mixed them up.

ZEF (*pausing the game*). Up, up, down, down, left, right, left, right, B, A, Start. (*The blooping sound again. He unpauses*

the game.) Yes, mate, yes! Finally, we're unstoppable…
(*Blasts through alien spacecraft. To* NEIL.) Go high, go high!

NEIL. Got him.

NEIL *and* ZEF *lay waste to the alien craft for a moment.
Then –*

Did you see the news about Al-Mansur?

ZEF (*focused on the game*). Nope.

NEIL. They ruled her death a suicide.

ZEF. Okay. (*Re: the game*.) Left, left, left!

NEIL. Cora yelled at – (*Correcting himself*.) Cora Preece, the
journalist, yelled at the coroner during the verdict. Called
him a 'hack', said the whole thing was a 'cover-up', got
kicked out of the courtroom.

ZEF. Shit. She lost the plot a bit?

NEIL. Well… she has a point. Doesn't she?

ZEF *doesn't respond.*

I mean, you said it yourself, the timing's crazy, right? We go
dark, Ameera's dead within hours.

ZEF. Don't go all 'conspiracy nut' on me.

NEIL. I keep thinking… if we wanted to keep Al-Mansur quiet
– 'we' as in British Intelligence – why didn't we just arrest
her?

ZEF. Makes a lot of noise. Police, lawyers, everything on the
record.

NEIL. A BSS grab-team, then. Bring her in, threaten to deport
her unless she hands over the spreadsheet.

ZEF. Maybe that's what this was. MI5 grab-team who shit the
bed. They go in, Ameera panics, tries to climb down her
balcony. Then they act as surprised as the rest of us – to hide
their total fucking incompetence.

NEIL. Maybe. Or… it was the Saudis. Assassination team. Like
with Khashoggi.

ZEF. Wouldn't put it past 'em. (*Re: the game.*) Shit, shit, shit – go low, go low!

NEIL. On it. (*Then.*) But even if it was the Saudis – someone had to *tell* them Ameera was a threat, right? She's been living in London for, what, four years? Totally peacefully. Then we find out about the spreadsheet, and all of a sudden –

ZEF. Don't do that, mate – don't put this on us. This is the job. They ask us to find stuff, we find it, we pass it up the chain. What happens after that is…

NEIL. – Not our responsibility?

ZEF. Above our pay grade. (*Then.*) Mate, it's the weekend. Can we just shoot aliens?

NEIL. Yeah. Sure.

They blast away at the alien spacecraft, as –

CORA. What is it, Dee – what's the emergency?

Lights up on DENISE*'s office at the* Guardian, DENISE *behind her desk, sombre-faced, several sheets of paper laid out in front of her.* CORA *enters in a rush, with a notebook and a bottle of orange juice.*

Lights down on NEIL*'s bedroom.*

DENISE. Cora, hi. Take a seat.

CORA. Is this gonna take long? I want to get up to Hampstead nick by five, catch the DCI on his way out.

DENISE. Just… sit. Please.

CORA *reluctantly slumps down in a chair.*

CORA. Uh-oh. Am I about to get detention? (*Off* DENISE*'s dour expression.*) Is this about what's-his-name… Dr Novelty Socks.

DENISE. You mean Dr Barrett –

CORA. Yeah, look, it was nice of you guys to offer, but I told you – and I told him – I don't need therapy. I'm not sick –

DENISE. – What you went through was *trauma*, Cora –

CORA. – I'm angry. *Furious*. And the cure isn't whingeing to a stranger about my childhood – it's nailing the bastards who killed Ameera.

DENISE. He's helped a lot of people in that newsroom. Ask Saj, ask Anna –

CORA. I didn't go to Iraq, I was in Kensington. So thanks, but no thanks. (*Standing*.) Is that it, because I'm on the clock –

DENISE. Sit. (*Then*.) Paul got a letter this morning, from the Saudi Embassy. Or rather, from lawyers representing the Saudi Embassy. Apparently you've been writing to them?

CORA. Oh that. Yeah, I sent a letter or two.

DENISE. Half a dozen letters, demanding the release of information from their General Intelligence Directorate –

CORA. – about their actions regarding Ameera Al-Mansur, yeah. I want to know what they did, the night Ameera died. What's wrong with that?

DENISE. They've enclosed copies of your letters, Cora.

CORA. So?

DENISE (*reading*). '…Unless the *Guardian* is given access to the requested files, we will publish damaging information regarding senior members of the Saudi Royal Family.' (*Pause*.) Cora?

CORA. You have to play hard ball. Bluff a bit –

DENISE. They're suing us. The paper, the Trust, you personally.

CORA. Oh, come on…

DENISE. They're calling it blackmail, and they have a case – what on earth were you thinking?

CORA. I wanted to rattle their cage, looks like it worked. This is just bullying, right? Trying to scare us off –

DENISE. No. This is a devastating legal liability and it is *not* how we operate. I've been trying to support you on this story, but when you behave this… recklessly, you make that impossible.

CORA. If you need me to explain it to Paul, I'm happy to –

DENISE. Paul wants to fire you. (*Beat.*) I talked him down. But you will be suspended, starting right now. And you will be required – and I do mean *required* – to accept the treatment you need. Dr Barrett's recommended an excellent inpatient facility –

CORA. Oh, fuck off. First they call Ameera 'unstable', now you want to lock me up, too? For what – doing my job? (*Indicating the letter.*) These guys cut journalists up with bone saws. If we let them push us around, what does that say about us?

DENISE. What's in the bottle, Cora?

Beat.

CORA. Orange juice.

DENISE. Only orange juice?

CORA *stands, bottle clenched tightly in her fist.*

CORA. This is such bullshit, I can't believe you're attacking *me*...

DENISE. No one's attacking you – we want to help –

CORA. Well, you can shove your help, and your therapy, and your job. I'm gone. Problem solved.

DENISE. Don't, Cora. Don't let it end like this.

CORA *storms out of the office.*

Come back, talk to me – Cora? (*Then, to herself.*) Shit.

Lights rise on NEIL, *sitting at his desk, listening on headphones.*

(*To* NEIL.) I tried to call her. Dozens of times.

NEIL. I know.

DENISE. I visited her apartment, she never answered. Wouldn't reply to emails – she completely cut me out.

NEIL. It wasn't just you. She cut off communication with almost everyone – no social media, no calls to her family, stopped seeing friends. She pretty much went dark.

DENISE. Was she just… drinking?

NEIL. Not *just* drinking. She was still trying to solve Ameera's murder – but it was chaotic, unfocused. Angry phone calls to the police, drunken messages to the Home Office, threatening emails to MI5. Then even that stopped – her laptop and phone were switched off for days at a time, no battery, I couldn't even switch them on remotely. We're an electronic intelligence agency – if you don't use electronic devices, we're basically… blind.

DENISE. But you were still trying.

NEIL. Every day. I probably checked her devices more often than I checked my own email. For weeks there was nothing – complete blackout. Until the morning I got –

Ping! NEIL's *computer screen projects against the back wall. An alert box –* '**Target #819-658-562: device online.**'

ZEF. Mate, where you at with those server logs?

Lights rise on NEIL *and* ZEF's *office. Lights down on* DENISE.

NEIL *and* ZEF's *computer screens (projected behind them, as always) are filled with indecipherable logs from Linux servers – spreadsheets containing long lists of dates, times and IP addresses – as well as the alert on* NEIL's *screen*

NEIL (*to* ZEF). Almost done.

ZEF. I'm telling you this is a fat waste of our time. It's either the Russians or the Chinese, and either way – they're good enough to cover their tracks.

NEIL's *mouse hovers over the alert. He starts to type a command – then stops. Deletes it.*

Seriously, mate – are you copying out those server logs by hand?

NEIL (*to* ZEF). Sending the first batch through now.

ZEF. Finally.

NEIL *clicks 'Send' – then pulls on his headphones. Types out a command and –*

Lights up on CORA, *sitting on her sofa, laptop open in front of her.* CORA *looks a wreck, as does her apartment – dirty plates, junk-food packets, empty vodka bottles and orange juice cartons strewn around her.*

CORA*'s laptop screen is projected onto the wall behind her: a web browser, open at a standard search page.*

CORA (*to the audience*). Suicide methods.

On the screen, the cursor types into the search box: '**suicide methods**'. CORA *hits* '*Search*', *and brings up a page of results relating to suicide.*

NEIL (*staring at his screen*). No.

ZEF. What's that, mate?

NEIL. Nothing, nothing.

CORA. Painless suicide methods.

CORA*'s cursor taps out:* '**painless suicide methods**' *into the search box. Through what follows, everything* CORA *says will show up as a new web search. As she clicks through links, opens new tabs, her screen fills up with web pages relating to each search term –*

Drug overdose suicide failure rate. (*Beat.*) Why suicide overdose fails. (*Beat.*) Most effective suicide methods. (*Beat.*) Most lethal suicide methods. (*Beat.*) Purchase cyanide London.

NEIL. No no no.

CORA. Poisoning failure rate. (*Beat.*) Carbon monoxide suicide failure rate. (*Beat.*) Carbon monoxide poisoning effects. (*Beat.*) Hanging versus poisoning. (*Beat.*) Hanging methods. (*Beat.*) Is hanging painful. (*Beat.*) Time before unconscious hanging.

ZEF. Neil? You asleep, mate? I'm ready for the next server dump.

NEIL. Still working on it, just... give me a second, alright?

CORA. Hanging long drop versus short drop. (*Beat.*) Short-drop hanging method. (*Beat.*) Rope length required hanging.

(*Beat*.) Rope thickness required hanging. (*Beat*.) Climbing rope hanging. (*Beat*.) Climbing equipment stores London. (*Beat*.) Urban Rock Climbing store opening times.

CORA *clicks through to the website of the Urban Rock Climbing store, and begins sifting through the products.*

Rope and rope bags. (*Beat*.) Single ropes. (*Beat*.) Single ropes bestsellers.

CORA *slams her laptop shut. Lights down on* CORA. *The window on* NEIL*'s computer screen goes blank.*

NEIL (*under his breath*). Shit.

ZEF. Mate, have you got something you'd rather be doing? Because I can pull the logs myself, if –

NEIL (*to* ZEF). No, no, they're ready – I'm sending them over now.

ZEF. Ta.

NEIL *sends a document to* ZEF. *Ping! Another alert on Neil's screen: 'Target #819-658-562: cellphone online.' A map of London appears on* NEIL*'s screen, a red dot showing* CORA*'s location.*

NEIL (*to the audience*). GPS on her mobile showed she'd left her flat. Contactless payment on her debit card showed she was on the 217 bus towards White City. I watched her enter the Westfield shopping centre – where the Urban Rock Climbing store is located. I was pinged when her bank processed a debit-card transaction for Summit Wall-Master Rope, thirty metres. Fifty-nine pounds. A few minutes later, she stopped at Asda and picked up a bottle of Russian Standard Vodka. Then she's back on the bus. Then she's home. The internet searches pick up again –

Lights up on CORA*'s apartment, as she reopens her laptop. The window on* NEIL*'s computer shows* CORA*'s face as she googles the information she needs.*

CORA. Best knot hanging. (*Beat*.) Simple noose knot versus strangle snare. (*Beat*.) Video how to tie simple noose.

A length of brightly coloured climbing rope descends in front of CORA. *She takes one end, and begins trying out various noose knots – taking swigs from a bottle of vodka, in between attempts.*

NEIL (*to the audience*). I don't know what to do. She's doing everything so fast, and I… can't think what what the fuck to do. I turn on her webcam. I catch glimpses of her, I hear sounds. She's definitely got a rope. She's definitely tying it.

ZEF (*frustrated*). Okay, either your computer's broken, or your brain's broken, because it doesn't take this long to –

CORA *rips back a fingernail, trying to unpick a knot.*

CORA. OW. Fuck it.

CORA *slams her laptop shut. Lights down on* CORA.

NEIL (*standing*). Fuck!

Beat. ZEF *looks at* NEIL, *confused.*

ZEF. You got Tourette's, mate?

NEIL. I'm sorry, I just need to… There's something I need to… tell you. Right now. It's time-critical and you're… really not going to like it.

ZEF. Okay.

NEIL. We're friends, right, we can tell each other things?

ZEF. Course.

NEIL. So the thing is… here's the thing, is that this morning I've… For a little while now, actually, I've… been… (*Hesitates.*) suffering from stomach flu.

ZEF. Mate.

NEIL. And it's gotten really bad. Uncontrollable.

ZEF. That's it? I thought it was the end of the world – the look on your face…

NEIL. It's gotten so bad that I think – I really think I need to go home. I'm sorry, but it's been really constant, all morning. Out of both ends. Explosive, frankly –

ZEF. Yeah, yeah, enough details, thanks. Just go home, yeah? (*Indicating his screen.*) I can deal with this shit – you deal with yours.

NEIL (*grabbing his bag*). Thanks…

ZEF. Get well soon, mate. Sorry I was hassling you.

NEIL. Forget it.

NEIL *grabs his bike helmet and rushes to the door, leaving a baffled ZEF in his wake – the light fading on ZEF, as NEIL dashes centre-stage.*

(*To the audience.*) I knew it was stupid. Even as I ran through security – as fast as I could without actually getting shot – every scan, every metal detector, the whole time I'm thinking: she could be hanging herself, jumping off a chair, right now. Or now. Or now. But what the fuck can I do? She's in London, I'm in Cheltenham – who am I kidding? I should call someone – but who can I call, who won't raise questions? I jump on my bike, just to be doing *something*, you know? Forward motion. I'm going to London – I know that for certain. Even if I'm too late, even if all I end up doing is staring at her dead body – I am going to fucking London to face all this. It was quarter to one when I left Benhall. The next train's leaving in eight minutes' time. It's at least a ten-minute ride to the station, I don't stand a chance of making it. But I'm so full of adrenaline – I hit the pedals and don't stop. Out the security gate, round the roundabout, cars honking. Running red lights, people diving out of my way, I pedal, pedal, pedal. Screeching round the junction to the station – the train's already at the platform, doors already open. I jump off my bike – don't lock it up, just drop it in the road – and rush the barrier, no ticket, nothing in my mind except those train doors – starting to close. I fling an arm into the door and I just shove, hard as I can. The guard's whistling, people are shouting – but I shove the door back and I'm in. I'm on the train. And I just collapse against the wall for at least a minute, I almost pass out. When I can finally see again – when I get to my feet, my legs are rubber, I stagger to an empty table –

Lights rise on an empty train seat, which NEIL *collapses into.*

But what now? It's a two-hour train ride to London. More than that to her flat. I have to do something *now. (Then.)* Okay... crazy thought: I could call her. Directly. I could just talk to her. Tell her it's alright, tell her it's not her fault.

NEIL *takes out his mobile phone, starts tapping at the screen.*

If I mask my number... use voice-over-IP, encrypted connection... *(About to dial – but hesitates.)* But it'll only be encrypted at my end. Her phone's been compromised. Because *I fucking hacked it!*

NEIL *lowers his mobile phone.*

I'm not equipped to deal with this. I don't know what to do.

Lights down on NEIL.

Lights up on CORA *in her flat. The colourful noose now tied perfectly, a chair beneath it.*

CORA*'s sitting on her sofa, scribbling something onto a notepad on her lap. She pauses, reads back what she's written... and crosses something out. She scribbles something else. Crosses it out again.*

CORA. Fuck's sake.

CORA *pours the last of her vodka into a glass, then empties the dregs of a carton of orange juice on top of it. Swigs. Picks up the pen, tries again. Reads it back, starting to cry now.*

It'll do.

CORA *places the notepad on her coffee table – and notices all the mess on the table (cartons, plates, etc.). She starts tidying up, sweeping the trash into a waste-paper basket. She picks up the dirty plates and glasses, about to take them to her kitchen... but then throws those in the trash as well.*

Okay. *(Pause.)* Okay.

CORA *walks towards the noose. Climbs onto the chair. She yanks on the rope a couple of times, checking it's securely tied. She pulls the noose wide. Puts her head through it. Pulls it tight.*

She takes a breath. And another. Faster and faster, psyching herself up. She tries to step off the chair. Can't.

(*Softly, to herself.*) It's just a step…

She puts out a foot. About to step off, as –

– Her buzzer goes off. CORA*'s startled – grabbing the rope for support, looking towards her door. She waits. Silence.*

The buzzer goes again. CORA *waits. Long silence.* CORA *feels the noose around her neck. Tugs on the rope again, when –*

A loud banging at the door. A man's voice, loud –

DAVE (*through the door*). Hello? Is anyone there? Ambulance service, we were called to this address. Hello?

More banging on the door. CORA *is stunned.*

CORA (*calling*). Um. Hello?

MIKE (*off*). Paramedics, can you let us in please?

CORA *loosens the noose. Pulls her head out. Looks at the door, then back at the noose – 'What the fuck?'*

CORA. Er – I didn't call for a paramedic –

DAVE (*off*). This is flat nineteen?

CORA. Yes.

DAVE (*off*). We were called about somebody not breathing at this address. Can you let us in? We're here to help.

CORA. But there's… no one in trouble here. Everything's fine, it's all fine.

DAVE (*off*). Please can you let us in?

CORA. Er… I don't… I… Just a minute.

CORA *grabs the noose, and flings it up towards another beam in her ceiling – partially obscuring it from view.* DAVE *knocks again, as* CORA *hurriedly moves the chair, and shuts the notepad containing her suicide note.*

DAVE *(off)*. We can't go until we've spoken to you, I'm afraid. Please can you –

CORA *opens the door, to reveal two paramedics –* DAVE *and* RACHEL.

CORA. Hi, sorry, hi – I think there must have been some kind of mistake?

DAVE. I'm Dave, this is Rachel – what's your name?

CORA. It's… Cora.

DAVE. Can we come in, please, Cora?

CORA. Sure, sure, come in. It's just me, I'm home alone. I don't understand why you're here.

The paramedics enter the flat, looking around.

DAVE. Do you have a disabled relative, miss?

CORA. A… what? No.

RACHEL. Have you seen anyone… or heard anyone having breathing difficulties, this afternoon?

CORA. No. No one.

DAVE. Have you been drinking, miss?

CORA. What's that got to – it's my flat, I can… Look, I'm sorry you were called out for nothing – maybe it was a prank, or maybe… maybe they meant number nine? The lady in number nine, she's pretty old, quite frail.

The paramedics look at each other.

RACHEL. I'll go check it out.

RACHEL *exits as* DAVE *speaks into his radio.*

DAVE *(into radio)*. November three-oh-seven, we're at nineteen Merrick Court – no sign of anyone in distress, repeat, no emergency found. Can you confirm address? *(Heads for the door. To* CORA.*)* Thank you, miss, sorry to disturb.

CORA. No problem, I hope you... find what you're looking for.

> DAVE *exits.* CORA *stands a moment. She looks back at her flat – the hidden rope, the chair, the sofa. She looks out of her back window – did somebody see what she was doing?*
>
> *She sits down on the sofa, her hands shaking. She grabs the vodka bottle – but there's nothing left. She flings the bottle away in frustration. Covers her face with her hands*
>
> *She stands, grabs her wallet, phone and keys – and heads out of her flat.*
>
> *Music plays. The bustle of a bar on a Wednesday night.* CORA *sits on a stool at the bar (facing the audience) – ignoring the people around her, clutching a vodka with orange juice like it's holding her up.*
>
> *A man pushes through the crowd behind her, looking for someone.* NEIL, *backpack on his shoulder, wild-eyed, mobile phone clutched in his hand like a Geiger counter. He's moving too quickly, shoving, irritating the bar's clientele.*
>
> NEIL *stops dead when he sees* CORA *at the bar. Stares a moment, like he can't believe she's real. Breathes with deep relief.* NEIL *looks around the bar again – 'What do I do now?' He stands a long moment, at a loss about his next step.*
>
> *The bar FREEZES – the music stops. Spotlight on* NEIL.

NEIL (*to himself/the audience*). Oh God. Oh God. She's alive, mission accomplished – go, get out, now. (*Starts to leave. Stops.*) But... what if she tries again? What if she goes home and... fuck. You've got to say something. Make it better. (*Then.*) But I can't talk to strangers. According to multiple diagnostic questionnaires, my social skills are below average – I say the wrong thing, I upset people, I don't mean to, it just happens. Can't risk it. (*Turns to leave again. Stops.*) But... she's not a stranger. I don't have to guess what makes her happy, parse her facial expressions for microscopic cues, I... I know the answers. This is god mode. (*Under his breath.*) Up, up, down, down, left, right, left, right, B, A, Start.

The bar unfreezes, music playing. NEIL *strides up to the bar, stands next to* CORA.

(*To the barman.*) Up.

CORA *looks across at* NEIL, *quizzically. Raises her own glass –*

CORA. Man of taste. Don't meet many guys who drink screwdrivers.

NEIL. Up.

CORA. Ha. My thoughts exactly. Vitamin C *and* alcohol – it's basically a health drink.

A screwdriver appears in front of NEIL. *He picks it up, raises it in a toast.*

NEIL. Down.

CORA (*a weak smile, raising her glass*). And to yours.

They drink. CORA *drains her glass completely.*

NEIL. Down?

CORA. Oh, that's sweet of you, but I don't accept drinks from strangers.

NEIL. Left.

CORA. Well, now there you make an excellent point. (*Calling to the barman.*) Phil? Two screwdrivers, please – doubles. This gentleman says it's more efficient if you make both at once.

Two new screwdriver cocktails appear at the bar. CORA *raises her glass –*

To efficiency.

They clink glasses, drink.

I'm Cora, by the way.

NEIL. Left. (*Panicked.*) Fuck, I mean… right.

CORA. Wow, you really had to think about that one, Tom. You sure that's only your second drink?

NEIL. Left.

CORA. Well, that makes two of us. And before you ask – no, I don't want to talk about it.

NEIL. Right.

CORA (*smiling*). Deal. I won't ask about your shitty day, you don't ask about mine.

NEIL. B.

CORA. Glad we understand each other.

NEIL. A.

CORA (*laughing*). To forgetting.

NEIL. Start.

The pace starts to accelerate – we're seeing scattered moments from their night in the bar. CORA*'s getting more drunk with each interaction:*

CORA. Yeah, I've told him a thousand times – (*Calling to the barman.*) Phil? (*Indicating* NEIL.) My friend thinks the music sucks too. Do you have anything decent back there? And two more screwdrivers.

NEIL. Up.

CORA (*stunned, but pleased*). Shut the fuck up – you know Jai Paul?

NEIL. Up.

CORA. No, I do not *like* Jai Paul. I love him. In a way which transcends the musical and enters the realms of the sexual. (*Raising her glass.*) Here's to having great taste.

NEIL. Down.

CORA (*tipsy*). Exactly. Exactly. I deleted my Facebook account months ago, for that exact reason. I mean, you don't change the world, you don't effect real, lasting political change, by clicking a fucking 'Like' button.

NEIL. Down.

CORA. Yeah, yeah – I agree completely. Sugar, news, sex – this stuff's supposed to be scarce, that's what we're wired for. If our brains haven't evolved to handle Coca-Cola – they *definitely* haven't evolved to handle Tinder.

NEIL. Left.

CORA *(laughing)*. Okay, that's bad – but I can top it. I once had a guy send me five unsolicited dick pics – five – with a tape measure in every shot. You know, 'for scale'.

NEIL. Um. Right.

CORA. Oh, me too, I deleted all my dating apps. But without them, I mean... it's like travelling back in time, right? What are you left with? Find a partner from your dwindling pool of single friends, or die alone. *(Calling.)* Phil? Screwdrivers.

NEIL. Left.

CORA *(drunk)*. I guess it's... *this*, right? *(Indicates the bar.)* Before all the dating apps, this is what people had. Hang around a bar, wait for a handsome guy to buy you a drink, and hope he makes you laugh. *(Quickly.)* Not that that's... I'm not saying we're... I mean, I expect you have... someone waiting for you?

NEIL. Right.

CORA. Oh. Me neither.

CORA *sips her drink. Lets the moment hang.*

NEIL. Er... B.

CORA. You're kidding – Bristol? Tonight? But tha's miles away! How the hell are you gonna... do trains even leave after midnight?

NEIL. A.

CORA. Shit, tha's awful – I'm sorry, 's my fault you missed it. No, no, no, don't do that, don't waste money on some shitty Travelodge or whatever... Nope, nope, I won't let you. I made you miss your train, and I've got this perfec'ly good sofa, so if you need a place to crash, s'the least I can do. Come on, seriously. Less go.

CORA *steps off her stool – but stumbles a little, grabs onto* NEIL *for support.*

I'm okay, I'm okay. But I might just keep hold of an arm. My place is jus' round the corner, it's only like a two-minute walk... or a five-minute stagger. Let's make a... let's make a...

NEIL *looks out at the audience.*

NEIL. Start.

Dim lights rise on CORA*'s flat – deserted, exactly as it was when we last saw it. We hear voices from the hallway outside, through the front door. The jangle of keys dropping to the floor –*

CORA (*off*). Shit, dropped my keys. (*Then.*) I've got it, I've got it. I've opened doors before.

We hear the keys being picked up again. The click of a lock turning – and CORA *opens the door, flicking on the light as she enters.*

Told you it was a mess.

NEIL *enters behind her – hesitant, his satchel in one hand, a plastic shopping bag in the other. He looks around, wide-eyed, taking in the reality of a room he's only seen through webcams.*

NEIL. It's a... beautiful flat. Amazing view.

CORA. It's a shoebox, but this is London.

NEIL. No, it's much bigger than I thought – (*Quickly.*) than I imagined, based on how you described it. I'm... so grateful to you, letting me crash here.

CORA. Enough 'thank-yous' – it's only a sofa. You make yourself comfortable, while I – (*Grabs the plastic bag from* NEIL.) fix us that nightcap.

CORA *heads to her kitchenette, pulling two bottles of wine out of the plastic bag.*

NEIL. We really don't have to drink more, if you... I mean, if you don't want to –

CORA. I promised drinks, and drinks we shall have. Here – (*Plugs her phone into a speaker.*) choose some music.

NEIL. Um, sure. What do you want to listen to?

CORA. Surprise me.

CORA *checks her cupboard for clean glasses. Can't find any. Grabs some mugs instead.* NEIL *scrolls through the music on her phone – finds what he's looking for, hits play.*

Oh, shit yes. Perfect choice. Turn it up. (*Dances around her kitchenette.*) I want you to know: I never do this. Invite strange men back to my place after one drink. Or five drinks. Not that sort of girl.

NEIL. I know. (*Quickly.*) I mean, you don't seem like that sort of... I also, I don't usually... buy drinks for strange girls. By which I mean girls who are strangers. To me.

CORA. I also don't usually drink – (*Scrutinises bottle.*) 'Cook's Choice Wine-Based Drink', but it's been a day of firsts – (*Dropping a mug.*) SHIT.

The mug clatters into CORA*'s sink.*

NEIL. You alright?

CORA. Fine, fine. No use crying over spilt Liebfraumilch.

She grabs another mug, fills it up. Half-dances, half-stumbles over to NEIL. *Hands him a drink. Takes a gulp of her own.*

Oooh, that's nasty. That is nasty.

NEIL. We don't have to drink it, if –

CORA. No, no, it's perfect. Noxious end to a noxious day.

NEIL (*cautiously*). Anything you want to... talk about?

CORA. Oh, sure, that's what you want, right? Listen to my problems, while I sob hysterically.

NEIL. I don't mind.

CORA (*scrutinising him*). You don't, do you? (*Pause.*) I... (*Stops herself.*) Forget it. Life's too short. And if it's not... (*Raises her glass.*) there's always suicide, right?

She clinks her glass against his, swigs her drink.

NEIL. I don't know if I want to drink to that.

CORA. Oh, come on. Never had a day when you wanted to curl up and die?

NEIL. Sure, of course I've… I mean, everyone does. But I think… in the end I think… the people who want to curl up and die… are usually the people the world needs more of.

CORA. Not sure I agree with you there, Tom.

NEIL. Think of all the… Sylvia Plaths, the van Goghs, the Scott Hutchisons…

CORA. Jeffrey Epstein, Hitler…

NEIL. Okay, there are some exceptions, but… most of the time, I think maybe it's the worst kinds of people – the narcissistic, the cruel – who never question their right to exist. Which implies, logically speaking, that if you're thinking about killing yourself… odds are you're someone who shouldn't do it. Because the world needs more of you.

CORA *looks away.*

Sorry – did I – ?

She kisses him – almost aggressively. Pushes him backwards towards the bed in the corner.

Are you sure –

CORA (*kissing him*). Sssh.

NEIL. I don't think –

CORA (*another kiss*). Shut up.

She shoves NEIL back onto the bed, landing on top of him. NEIL melts into it for a moment… then pulls away. Gently presses CORA back –

NEIL. Cora –

CORA. Enough talking, please can we just –

She tries to kiss him again, but NEIL pulls back.

Oh. You… don't like me? I thought –

NEIL. Of course I like you, I think you're... perfect, honestly.

CORA. I'm a long fucking way from perfect –

NEIL. I disagree. And that's why I want to... I mean, I don't want to... like this.

CORA. Like what? I'm not *that* drunk –

NEIL. I just... I don't feel right about... I should take the sofa. If that's still okay.

CORA looks into NEIL's eyes, trying to gauge whether she's being brushed off.

CORA. Perfect?

NEIL. Yes.

They kiss again – more gently this time. They break, look into each other's eyes.

I'll... be on the sofa.

NEIL stands, makes his way to the sofa, as CORA turns onto her side, watching him go – still trying to read him.

CORA. You're either a very good man... or a very strange one, Tom Flowers.

NEIL smiles at her, but doesn't reply.

I'm just gonna... rest my face for a minute.

CORA slumps forwards onto her bed. Passes out.

NEIL watches CORA for a long moment, as her breathing deepens. He quietly pads back to the bed, tries to pull the duvet over her... but she's passed out on top of it. After a moment's thought, NEIL gently folds the duvet over her like a taco.

He searches for the light switches, turns down the lights. Pads his way to the sofa. Sits, exhausted.

NEIL (*freaking out*). What am I doing? What have I done? (*Then.*) Okay, okay, okay, this is... this is fixable, it's... probably fixable. I mean – (*Indicating CORA.*) she's not dead, so that's... that's something. And she seems to... I mean, she... *likes* me. I think. And that's... new.

NEIL *rubs his eyes. Leans back into the sofa. Closes his eyes a moment. A thought hits him – he sits up abruptly.*

No. Cora doesn't like *me* – she likes Tom Flowers. A fictional network security consultant, working for a fictional IT company with no website, no address, and no social-media presence of any kind. Tomorrow she's probably going to google 'Tom Flowers', and she's going to find – nothing. At all. Which is really suspicious. And she's... I mean despite all this, she's still a journalist. She knows me now, knows my face – if she figures out who I really am... if any of this ever came out... she could burn the whole agency to the ground. A total, undeniable, catastrophic breach of operational security. Bollocks. Bollocks bollocks bollocks. Tom Flowers needs... a life.

NEIL *grabs his laptop from his satchel, opens it up.*

Through what follows, NEIL*'s computer screen projects on the back wall – as he blasts through a blizzard of website-building tools, social-media account set-up pages, stock photography websites, etc. –*

Alright, start with the basics – Facebook page, Instagram account. Set both accounts to private, obviously, but I still need profile pictures and I can't use anything which will trigger facial recognition. So Tom Flowers' profile photos happen to be... (*Scrolls through his personal photo collection.*) wearing a mask and snorkel, and... wearing ski-goggles. Yeah. Tom Flowers likes sports. (*Then.*) Tom Flowers' Instagram posts consist of... photos from bicycle rides in the Bristol area, cloned from defunct Flickr pages –

... as he speaks, NEIL *is dragging photographs from someone else's Flickr account into his new Instagram account, adding his own personal captions –* ... **'Twenty-five miles today!!'** ... **'#newbicycle'** ... **'Sunset on the downs. #lovebristol'** ...

– none of which show his face. Tom's Facebook page consists mostly of shared articles supporting progressive causes. Because Tom Flowers cares passionately about... (*Selecting articles.*) the wage gap... and the environment.

Finally, Tom needs friends for these accounts – which should be difficult to fake, but isn't, because Russian spambot accounts are easy to identify, and they're guaranteed to 'friend' me back. So I spam the spammers – three hundred friend requests to every fake account I can find. And just like that… Tom Flowers is popular.

On screen, Tom Flowers' Facebook page rapidly racks up over a hundred friends.

Next up, corporate web page for Tom's company. A company whose name I made up back at the bar after a *lot* of drinking, and now… can't remember. It was… (*Struggles to remember.*) something… like… Net… Vault… Tech? Net Vault Tech. God, that's terrible.

Onscreen, NEIL's quickly registering domain names – 'netvaulttech.com', 'netvaulttech.net'…, etc. The screen then fills with HTML code, as NEIL steals text from another website –

Okay, clone the website from a real IT consultancy, fiddle the CSS sheet, change the address, switch out real employee names for fakes. Place Tom Flowers on the 'Our Experts' page, then hammer the meta tags and anchors on every page, so the real company will never find the copy on Google, but it'll come up quickly for anyone searching for Tom Flowers. A fake address on a real Bristol street, fake phone number which forwards to my mobile after multiple redirects, a Gmail account – tomflowers100@gmail.com – and a final flourish –

NEIL*'s screen fills with charity fun-run pages –*

– a JustGiving charity page for a five-kilometre run in aid of… Great Ormond Street Hospital. (*Hits 'Enter' triumphantly.*) Aaaand – Boom. (*Collapses back into the sofa – exhausted.*) Tom Flowers is a real boy. And it's 8 a.m.. And I haven't slept. (*Takes a breath.*) Okay. Exit strategy.

Behind NEIL*, the sun is rising. He closes the laptop. Stands. Heads into the kitchenette.*

CORA *stirs on the bed. Winces at the sunlight. Struggles to get her arms out of the folded duvet. She groans, rubs her head, moving gingerly.*

CORA (*croaking*). Mor… (*Clears her throat.*) Morning.

NEIL *reaches into the oven – removes a baking tray with fresh pastries on it.*

NEIL. Morning. (*Checking the time.*) Just.

CORA (*squinting at the light*). Are you… cooking?

NEIL. I went out for pastries – left the door on the latch, I hope that's okay? (*Indicating the baking tray.*) Just warming them up.

CORA *pulls on a hoodie – suddenly self-conscious about her appearance. Scrapes her hands through her hair while he's not looking, trying to tame it.* NEIL *carries the pastries over to the bed.*

They were out of croissants, I got something called a… cinnamon social slice?

CORA. *Shut up.* (*Then.*) You went to Dominique's?

NEIL. Is that… bad?

CORA *grabs a pastry, takes a bite.*

CORA. Mm. Mmm. (*Mouth full.*) It's my favourite place in London and this… (*Another bite.*) this is the best thing they sell. (*Chewing.*) You're scoring *so* many points right now.

NEIL. Glad to hear it.

CORA (*scrutinising* NEIL). Who *are* you?

Beat.

NEIL. Didn't we… do this last night?

CORA (*playful*). Have you done this before? The whole 'Oops, I missed my train', thing – is that a line you use on vulnerable women?

NEIL. I can say with one-hundred-per-cent certainty, that I have never done this before. And I will need to catch that train some time soon, so…

CORA. Oh – you have to go?

Beat.

NEIL. Well, I mean... I should leave you to get on with your weekend.

CORA. Sure. I get it. You've got plans?

NEIL. You know, the usual weekend stuff that... people do... in Bristol. Maybe a bike ride. See some friends.

CORA. But nothing specific?

NEIL. Not set in stone, no.

CORA. It's just... I was going to say – and this is probably the breakfast talking, but – I was going to say... Do you want to hang out today? (*Beat.*) I'll have a shower, and everything, I have other clothes –

NEIL. No, no, it's not that, it's just... I don't... know if I should –

CORA. You just said you don't have any – (*A little exasperated.*) Okay, I'm confused, which of these mixed signals am I supposed to... I mean, you said you were single, but if that was bullshit then –

NEIL. No, I'm really... extremely single.

CORA. Alright. Well, I won't beg, but I'd... like to... not be alone today. (*Beat.*) Stay. Please?

A moment, then –

DENISE. What in God's name were you thinking?

Spotlight on DENISE, *scowling at* NEIL. *Lights down on* CORA.

NEIL. I was thinking... psychological studies of people who've survived a suicide attempt show –

DENISE. Don't give me more statistics, I'm asking about *you* –

NEIL (*persisting*). – *The studies show* that most survivors are 'glad' they didn't die. People who jump off the Golden Gate Bridge have a ninety-eight-per-cent chance of killing themselves. But people who *survived* the attempt –

DENISE. You're avoiding the question –

NEIL. – or were prevented from jumping – ninety-three per cent of them *didn't try again*. They were still alive, decades later. The crisis passes, the suicidal thoughts diminish, but it can take up to twenty-four hours.

DENISE (*acidly*). Oh, so you'd be 'saving' her, if you stayed?

NEIL. Distracting her.

DENISE. And the fact that a beautiful woman found you attractive – that didn't even enter your mind?

NEIL (*irritated*). I wouldn't risk my life for... that.

DENISE. 'Risk your life'? You're not James Bond, you work in an office – what are you going to die from, paper cuts?

NEIL. Stephen Drinkwater, 1983.

An image of a young man slumped in a chair projects against the back wall, a plastic bag fastened tightly around his neck with a thick rubber band.

GCHQ clerk, found dead in his parents' home, with a plastic bag over his head. Cause of death: asphyxiation.

A new image appears beside the first – an older man slumped in a chair, wearing women's lingerie. He, too, has a plastic bag fastened over his head.

Nicholas Husband, 1997. GCHQ computer scientist, found dead in his own home, wearing women's lingerie, with a plastic bag over his head. Cause of death: asphyxiation.

A third image appears, a man in his thirties, lying prostrate on a bed wearing boxer shorts, a plastic bag over his head, a painter's dusk mask pulled on top of the bag.

Kevin Allen, 1999, GCHQ linguist. You guessed it – plastic bag, asphyxiation. And then we get to the *really* dark one.

Spotlight on a large red duffel bag, the zips sealed with a bronze padlock.

Gareth Williams, 2010. GCHQ mathematician. Found decomposing in a bathtub, his naked body stuffed inside a red duffel bag with the zips padlocked together. In every case, the police found 'no signs of foul play'. They even claimed – with a straight face – that Gareth Williams 'probably did this to himself'. My employer has a very real problem with staff retention.

DENISE. And with bags.

NEIL. So yes, we're geeks, yes, we sit at computers all day, yes, we barely ever leave Cheltenham, but we are still, when it comes down to it, spies.

DENISE. Alright, you've made your point.

NEIL. And *that's* what I was thinking. The only logical choice was to extricate myself, as delicately as possible, as fast as possible.

The lights rise on CORA, *back in the moment we left hanging –*

CORA. I won't beg, but I'd... like to... not be alone today. (*Beat.*) Stay. Please?

NEIL *looks up at the photos of the dead men. The duffel bag. Then back at* CORA.

NEIL. Sure. I'd love to.

Lights down.

End of Act One.

ACT TWO

Spotlight on HANNAH, *facing the audience.*

HANNAH. Westminster Bridge, March 22nd 2017.

A projection screen flickers to life behind HANNAH, *showing press photos of urban carnage – the aftermath of the Westminster Bridge terror attack.*

A rented SUV mounts the kerb and ploughs into pedestrians – injuring fifty, five of them fatally. The driver emerges with a knife, fatally stabbing a policeman, before being shot by an armed protection officer.

The images change – to photos of chaos outside Borough Market.

Three months later, London Bridge. A white van, this time – runs over pedestrians, before three men emerge with kitchen knives, stabbing anyone within reach. Eight people killed, forty-eight injured.

The images change again – the London Bridge attack of November 2019.

Two years later: same bridge. Another aspiring terrorist wearing a fake suicide vest stabs five people, two of them fatally.

The screen goes blank.

We watch these attacks unfold on our screens, and we know – this should never have happened. These aren't just 'tragedies' – they are failures. It's our job to keep this country safe, and when we fail at that fundamental task, we need to ask ourselves – why? Why did we fail?

Images of the perpetrators of the attacks – Khalid Masood, Khuram Shazad Butt, Rachid Redouane, Usman Khan, Youssef Zaghba – project behind HANNAH.

Because the nature of the terrorist threat has changed. These men didn't attend Al-Qaeda camps, or fight in Syria: you're looking at a pastry chef, a gym receptionist, an English teacher, a benefit fraudster and an employee of Kentucky Fried Chicken. These are 'lone wolves', radicalised by websites and YouTube videos. Which means it's no longer enough for us to monitor ISIS commanders, or intercept chatter from the Middle East. When an attack can emerge from anywhere, we need to monitor *everyone*. As our Director says: 'We can't find the needles, unless we collect the whole haystack.' Which is why...

The images change again – a vast underground data-storage centre, row after row of server cabinets extending in every direction.

... we built *this*. The BFDC – Big Fucking Data Centre. Director Hatcher's signature project. The largest network of servers and supercomputers ever assembled on British soil, drawing enough electricity to power a small city. A rolling buffer of every click, search, tweet, email, text message, and transaction that passes through this country's fibre-optic cables. The biggest investment ever made in this agency, based on a single, simple promise: to identify 'lone wolf' terrorists, and stop them before they strike.

*The image shifts again – a complex 'org chart' of the agency's myriad data sources – dozens of boxes with impenetrable codenames and acronyms ('**FALLOUT**', '**CONVEYANCE**', '**NUCLEON**'...), connected by a spiderweb of lines. [Note: slides leaked by Edward Snowden will provide a basis for these.]*

We're supposed to sift through this vast haystack, flag potential terrorists, and pass them on to BSS for further investigation. But right now, we're flagging so *many* people – literally thousands per day – that BSS can't begin to follow them up. Because the system processing all this data is, not to put too fine a point on it...

*A new slide – a flowchart, even more incomprehensible than the last. Database jargon ('**keyword scoring**', '**merge strings**', '**cluster/factor**'...) connected with looping arrows, 'IF/THEN' statements, etc.*

… a colossal fucking mess. Over one hundred overlapping programmes and algorithms, cobbled together on an ad hoc basis over the course of the past two decades. After every terrorist attack, we write new modules, graft them onto the old ones. The end result is an opaque, unstable system, which crashes constantly. The IT guys call it 'the hornet's nest' – because it's full of bugs, and we're terrified to touch it. Which…

Lights up on a new office – the desks arrayed with multiple state-of-the-art computer monitors on reticulating arms. Digital whiteboards, etc. NEIL and ZEF are sitting on sleek ergonomic office chairs, watching HANNAH's presentation.

… is where you come in.

NEIL *and* ZEF *look at each other, confused.*

NEIL. Us, ma'am?

HANNAH. You, ma'am. I need you to audit the system, identify the weakest components, and replace them – fast. Get that false-positive number down. Start flagging actual terrorists, stop flagging every poor sod who uses an internet café in Birmingham. Our agency's reputation – and future funding – are on the line.

ZEF (*in disbelief*). Wait, sorry, ma'am, we're… moving to Counter-Terror?

HANNAH. Of course. The brand-new office wasn't a clue?

NEIL *and* ZEF *look around the office, stunned.*

ZEF. I thought we were just borrowing their chairs.

HANNAH. As of this morning, you work here – reporting directly to me. We're still working on the official title for your team – you were going to be 'Special Target Discovery', till we looked at the acronym. So for now you're 'Target Discovery, Special Ops'. (*Indicating their computers.*) We've upgraded your workstations, of course – twelve-core, i9, direct link to the HPC cluster.

ZEF (*gazing at his workstation*). Shut the front door.

HANNAH. You've got two months to make tangible, measurable improvements to this system, or the whole project's at risk – and half our funding with it.

ZEF. We won't let you down, ma'am.

NEIL. It won't work.

Beat.

HANNAH. I beg your pardon?

NEIL. This system: it's never going to work. We could rewrite the code all year – it won't make a difference. Because the code isn't the problem.

ZEF (*warning*). Mate…

HANNAH. And what *is* the problem, in your opinion?

NEIL. The entire concept. It's a classic base-rate fallacy. (*Off her blank look.*) A false-positive paradox.

HANNAH. In English?

NEIL. When you test a large population for a very rare condition – like, say, 'being a terrorist' – your test needs to be as accurate as the condition is rare. Otherwise you're guaranteed to get swamped with false positives.

HANNAH. Which is why you're going to *improve* the accuracy –

NEIL. It won't make a difference. You're searching for a few thousand terrorists, in a population of, what, sixty-six million people? If you have even a one-per-cent false-positive rate – which would be spectacular, by the way – you'll end up falsely accusing – (*Scribbling*) sixty-six thousand innocent people, for every *one* terrorist you accurately detect. It's worse than no test at all.

HANNAH (*with venom*). So what do you suggest we do? Sit around waiting for the next explosion, the next stabbing?

NEIL. That would arguably be a better use of / resources –

ZEF (*cutting* NEIL *off*). What Neil means is – there are formidable conceptual challenges here, we'll need a little time to digest all this. But we can *absolutely* improve on the current system, and get the false positives down. No question.

HANNAH. That's all I need from you. I know it won't be 'the perfect system', no one expects that. We just need something better than – (*Indicating the screen.*) this. We need to show *progress*. Understood?

ZEF. Yes, ma'am.

HANNAH. Neil?

NEIL *considers arguing – but catches* ZEF *staring daggers at him.*

NEIL (*reluctantly*). Yes, ma'am.

HANNAH. Good lads. Figure something out. I'm counting on you.

HANNAH *exits.* ZEF *punches the air in celebration –*

ZEF. Counter-Terror! Counter! Fucking! Terror! And you nearly *blew it*, you absolute spanner. (*Off* NEIL*'s dour look.*) This is it, mate, the big leagues! Are you gonna smile at some point, or is that against the Vulcan Code?

NEIL (*quietly*). Vulcan Axioms.

ZEF. Twat. (*Then.*) Can you please, for once in your life, be a bit less… *Neil* about all this?

A moment, then –

CORA. You're a fat fucking liar, Tom Flowers.

Lights up on CORA*, dressed for a night out, sitting at a bar table with two drinks. Loud music playing, the buzz of a bar in full swing.*

NEIL *steps into the scene with her, as the lights fade on the office.*

NEIL. Sorry?

CORA. You heard me: fat fucking liar. (*Then.*) You said you couldn't ice-skate.

NEIL (*relieved*). I can't.

CORA. If you don't fall down even once, you can ice-skate. Admit it – you take all the girls skating.

NEIL. Hardly. We don't have an ice rink in – (*A second's hesitation*.) Bristol.

CORA. Really?

NEIL. Not that I'm aware of.

CORA. Weird. My cousin went to Bristol Uni – I could've sworn he played ice hockey.

NEIL. Oh. Yeah. No, you're right – I think I have seen ads for an ice rink –

CORA. Busted!

NEIL. – but I've never been. Cross my heart.

CORA (*playful*). So his story keeps changing. First the rink doesn't exist, then it *does* exist but he's never gone there… Our readers demand the truth. You take a new girl ice-skating every night –

NEIL. I deny those reports completely…

CORA. – you get her all hot and bothered with your triple-axels and your pirouettes. Then you lead her back to your tawdry bachelor pad –

NEIL. Fake news.

CORA. – with the circular bed and the mirrors on the ceiling. Only to toss her out onto the street in the morning, with nothing but her leg warmers to cover her shame.

NEIL. Alright, alright, you've got me – I'm no match for your journalistic wiles. I confess: my real name is – (*Adopting a comical Russian accent*.) Boris Poplopovich, I am professional Russian figure skater, and FSB Intelligence Officer…

CORA. Finally, the truth.

NEIL. I sneak into this country on forged passport, on secret mission to seduce world's leading ice-dancing journalist – the dangerous but beautiful Cora Preece.

CORA. Ex-journalist.

NEIL. Still beautiful. And great threat to the morale of our Olympic team.

CORA. First you meddle in our elections – now this. Well, let me tell you something, Boris. Your vicious plan to seduce this paragon of ex-journalistic integrity... (*Leans in close.*) is working.

They kiss. Smile as they separate. CORA *knocks back her drink. Stands.*

We'll continue your interrogation at my apartment.

NEIL. You'll never break me.

CORA. We'll see.

CORA *takes his hand, starts to lead* NEIL *off, as –*

ZEF. Thoughts?

Lights up on ZEF, *standing at a digital whiteboard – staring at a meticulously drawn but incredibly messy flowchart, hundreds of arrows and acronyms (some scribbled out, some covered with question marks).*

NEIL. You first.

NEIL *steps into the office with* ZEF.

ZEF. I think... we're fucked.

NEIL. Anything more substantial?

ZEF. We are substantially fucked. (*Indicating the whiteboard.*) You were right. They might as well look for terrorists by throwing darts at a fucking census. There's no architecture here, no plan, it's just a giant pile of spaghetti. It'll take months to map it out, never mind improve it –

NEIL. What if we don't bother?

Beat.

ZEF. Come again?

NEIL. We don't bother mapping it out. This system's a mess, we know it doesn't work – why waste time unpicking it?

ZEF. Because… that's literally what we're here to do?

NEIL. Not true. We need to *improve* on this system. So, step one – throw the whole thing out. Step two, start from scratch –

ZEF (*dripping sarcasm*). Oh, sure, we'll just build a whole new system – that'll be *much* quicker.

NEIL. We let the system build itself. Neural network. Deep learning.

A beat as ZEF considers this.

ZEF. Okay, first question, seems like an obvious one, but – have you ever actually built a neural network?

NEIL. I've read some papers.

ZEF. Course you have.

NEIL. It's how Amazon cracked speech recognition. How banks spot bad credit risks –

ZEF. Yeah, and that took them *years* –

NEIL. But now they've done it, we don't need reinvent the wheel. We just borrow theirs.

ZEF *looks uneasy*

ZEF. Mate, as fun as that sounds… I don't know the first thing about neural nets. And that ain't gonna change much in a few weeks. I won't be any use to you.

NEIL. Bullshit. Remind me, you graduated *where* in your year?

ZEF. That was uni –

NEIL. Top of your year, undergrad and masters. So how many third-rate hacks are coding neural nets for Facebook, Apple, bloody… *Sainsbury's*, right now? Do you honestly think they can do it, and we can't?

ZEF *mulls this over.*

ZEF. Fuck it. I'll try.

NEIL. There he is. (*Tapping his keyboard.*) I'll send you some papers, get you up to speed.

ZEF *looks at* NEIL, *quizzically.*

ZEF. Mate, what's gotten into you? On Monday you're moping for Britain, today you're the love-child of John von Neumann and Kanye West. New medication?

NEIL (*smiling*). New outlook.

CORA. I had this irrational attack of optimism, after I last saw you.

Lights up on CORA*'s apartment – much tidier than before, the clutter cleared away. An open bottle of wine on the gleaming kitchen counter.* NEIL *slides his office chair across the stage, stepping off it, and into her flat.*

NEIL (*marvelling at the clean flat*). Bloody hell – what happened here?

CORA. Went through two rolls of bin bags, three bottles of Dettol, and I pretty much killed the hoover. But I just thought – fresh start, you know?

NEIL. Hey, this countertop's *white*, I never knew that.

CORA. Unblocked the sink, descaled the kettle, napalmed the fridge – for two whole days I was a laser beam of undiluted purpose. No moping, no weeping, no drinking – 'I'm gonna dust off my CV, apply for some jobs, *carpe* the bloody *diem.*'

NEIL. That's fantastic.

CORA. Then I tried to write my CV. And I started crying. And I couldn't stop. And I went to bed.

CORA *slumps onto the couch, knocks back her wine.* NEIL *sits next to her.*

NEIL. Hey…

CORA. I thought – 'Who am I kidding?' Why should I get a 'fresh start'? That's just another way of saying: I've given up. 'Sorry, Ameera, I can't bring your killers to justice right now – I'm applying to be Social Media Engagement Officer at fucking Google.' (*Pours herself more wine.*) Sorry, I've been trying so hard to be… sunshine and rainbows. Sex and ice-skating. But I can only keep it up so long. Welcome to the Real Cora – I'm a fucking mess. Run for your life.

NEIL *reaches out to* CORA, *uncertain.*

NEIL. I'm not going anywhere…

CORA. You should. (*Then.*) I can't get past it. I thought I could, but… I can't. My friend is dead – because of me.

NEIL. Not because of you –

CORA. My ambition, my story, my fault.

NEIL. I don't think she'd see it that way –

COR (*sharply*). And you don't know the first fucking thing about it.

NEIL. That's true. I only know what you've told me. But I think… *if* you apply for a job – when you're ready, not before – that doesn't mean you're giving up. The opposite – it means you'll have more resources, to keep up the fight. How much use are you to Ameera, if you're starving in the street?

CORA. Like anyone would give me a job, in this state. If I ever made it to an interview – which I won't – when anyone asks why I left the *Guardian*, I'll either burst into tears or throw up.

NEIL. I'll help you. With the CV, the applications, we can do practice interviews –

CORA. You an expert in journalism interviews?

NEIL. I like learning new things – it'll be fun. And you'll walk into a new job – there isn't a newsroom in this country that wouldn't be lucky to have you.

CORA *looks at* NEIL.

CORA. Why are you so nice to me?

NEIL. Because… you're the best person I've ever met.

CORA *manages a half-smile.*

CORA. You should meet more people.

ZEF. Zero-point-zero-zero-zero-one-three-per-cent probability.

Lights up on NEIL's *office.* ZEF's *at his desk.*

NEIL *jumps back into his office chair, slides back to his desk –*

NEIL. Probability of…?

ZEF. Me conspiring to commit a terrorist attack. According to the old system.

NEIL. You didn't run your own name…

ZEF. Course I did. Checked yours, too.

NEIL. Zef…

ZEF. Don't panic, lily-white – you're clean. Apparently I'm, like, four thousand times more likely than you to be wearing a suicide vest.

NEIL. Wow. So is this your way of confessing?

ZEF. It's my way of saying: the old system's a racist heap of garbage.

NEIL. Zef-sama bin Laden, under our noses this entire time.

ZEF. On the other hand – (*Indicating a pile on his desk.*) if it's a choice between reading more Bayesian stats papers, and waging global jihad, I might start taking chest measurements. Mate, this stuff's impenetrable.

NEIL. I can handle the Bayesian stuff, if you take the data-cleaning.

ZEF. You sure?

NEIL. Half my masters was Bayesian stats – I love that stuff.

ZEF. Legend. (*Off* NEIL*'s smile.*) Look at you – all giddy. What's going on with you, seriously? Did someone get lucky last night?

NEIL. No, nothing like that. Just… enjoying my work these days.

ZEF. Well, whatever's gotten into you – keep getting it.

CORA. These. Are. AMAZING.

NEIL *whizzes across the stage on his office chair – into* CORA*'s apartment. Through what follows, he hurtles back*

and forth between CORA*'s apartment and his office,*
juggling the two sides of his life.

The sample CVs you sent – where the hell did you get them
all? They're fantastic.

NEIL. Just… did a few web searches, nothing special.

CORA. Your web searches must be a *lot* better than mine.
Thank you.

ZEF. Christ on a jet-ski – have you seen these matching
modules?

NEIL *whizzes back across the stage, into his office.*

They're matching the names of terror suspects using fucking
Soundex.

NEIL. You're kidding me…

ZEF. Can't handle Arabic, can't handle Cyrillic… See, this is
the sort of thing that gives me hope. We can do better than
this, right?

NEIL. A masturbating chimpanzee could do better than this.

ZEF. Good thing you're on the team then.

NEIL *tosses an empty Red Bull can at* ZEF. *Then –*

NEIL. Before you write a new one from scratch – there's an
open-source Metaphone hybrid on GitHub. I'll send you
a link.

ZEF. My bloody hero.

CORA. So, the gaping hole in my CV where the last six months
should be…

NEIL *whizzes back across to* CORA.

… shall I just put 'drinking and weeping', or should I make
something up?

NEIL. How about… you put 'media consultancy' and put me
down as a reference.

CORA. No way – I can't. You could get fired for that –

NEIL. If anyone calls to check, I'll tell them you did an outstanding job.

CORA. You'd seriously… do that for me?

CORA *kisses him, delighted.*

ZEF. So either everyone in Cheshire's a terrorist…

NEIL *whizzes back to his office.*

… or our test run was a complete clusterfuck.

NEIL (*scrolling through the output*). It's the weights – we're initialising them with random values, they're not converging. Use the hard-coded values from the old model instead, they'll converge faster.

ZEF. Nice idea. But it'll take weeks to extract them all.

NEIL. Nah – I ran a bunch of refactoring tools, dumped all the variables in a database. Search by name, you should find what you're looking for pretty quickly.

ZEF. I could kiss you on the mouth. But Liz'd get jealous.

NEIL. How many times? I am not seeing Liz.

ZEF *looks at* NEIL, *suspicious.*

ZEF. That's a weirdly specific denial. '… Not seeing Liz.' So you admit you're seeing *someone*?

NEIL. I never said that –

ZEF. Oh my God – you are! I bloody knew it, you sneaky bastard. Who is she?

CORA. 'Business blouse' or 'funky dress'?

NEIL *whizzes back to* CORA*'s apartment – where she's holding up two outfits.*

On the one hand – (*Holding up the blouse.*) it's an editorial position. On the other hand – (*Holding up the dress.*) it's a digital start-up.

NEIL. I… have several talents. Fashion isn't one of them. Can you wear them together?

CORA (*turning away*). You're right – it was a mistake to ask.

NEIL. I'll say one thing. 'Funky dress' is kind of... cheeky.

CORA. Maybe I'll wear it tonight.

NEIL. Maybe I'd like that.

ZEF (*to* NEIL). Come on, out with it – who's the unlucky lady?

NEIL *whizzes back into the office –*

NEIL. If I tell you her name, you'll have her dirty photos downloaded in three seconds flat.

ZEF. Would I do that to you?

NEIL. Yes, you absolutely would.

NEIL *slides towards the centre of the stage – inhabiting both scenes at once, now.*

CORA. So when do I get to come up to Bristol?

NEIL (*to* CORA). Soon. When the building work's done – the flat's a bombsite at the moment.

ZEF. I'm not asking for her National Insurance number. Just the basics – where'd you meet, where's she work, what's her full name and date of birth? (*Then.*) Give me a first name, at least.

CORA. When do I meet your friends? You never talk about them...

NEIL (*to* ZEF). Karen. Her name's Karen. (*To* CORA.) Mostly I hang out with... Zac. A guy from work.

ZEF. Where did you meet?

CORA. How long have you known each other?

NEIL (*to* ZEF). A bar on the Promenade. She was visiting from Bristol. (*To* CORA.) We started work in the same year. Came up together. But he grew up there.

CORA. In Bristol?

ZEF. So that's where she's from – Bristol?

NEIL (*to both*). Yeah.

ZEF. If you won't show us a picture, at least describe her. Hair colour, dress size, cup size…

NEIL. No.

ZEF. Does she work out, or…?

NEIL. Bugger off.

CORA. Tom. Tom? (*Louder.*) Earth to Tom!

NEIL (*to* CORA). Hm? Sorry, I was miles away. What is it?

CORA. I swear I've had hamsters that answered to their name more reliably.

ZEF. Neil? Neil. NEIL.

NEIL (*rubbing his eyes, exhausted*). Mate, whatever it is – I'll get to it.

ZEF (*indicating his screen*). Have you seen these error logs? It's crashing every time we try the full sample. 'Exit code one-three-seven' –

NEIL. Zac, would you give me a break? I'll get to it.

Beat.

ZEF. Who's Zac?

NEIL. Sorry, mate, my brain's fried. (*Re: the error logs.*) It's a memory error – the float conversion's killing us every time.

CORA. I'm in Bath for a conference on Wednesday. I could come visit you! Get a good-luck kiss before my big interview, maybe do some more practice?

ZEF. Thames House are waiting for data – like, right now – we're nowhere near ready. We should cancel the test, ask for more time.

NEIL (*to* CORA). It's just bad timing. Ze– Zac and I are right up against it at work, we're sleeping in the office. (*To* ZEF.) The system's ready – it'll run. We just need to chunk the sample, run it through in batches.

CORA. Do I need to worry? Do you have, like, a wife and three kids out there – is that why you never let me visit?

ZEF (*exhausted, indicating his screen*). Mate, it's a disaster.
Look at this – we're barely sending through anything at all.

NEIL (*to* CORA). Soon, I promise. Just let me get through this
week, it's make-or-break for our whole project. But you're
gonna smash that interview, I know it.

CORA. It's going to be a catastrophe – I don't know why
I applied. I should cancel it.

ZEF. Told you we should've cancelled. Might as well put the
flags on postcards and mail them to Thames House, the rate
this thing's running.

NEIL (*shattered, to* ZEF). It's supposed to be conservative,
that's how we designed it. Main thing is – it's not crashing.
The system's ready. (*To* CORA.) Remember what we
practised, you'll knock 'em dead. I promise you – you're
ready for this.

HANNAH (*entering*). Alright, boys, the moment of truth.

NEIL *and* ZEF *share a queasy look, as* HANNAH *strides
into the office with a tablet computer.*

Lights down on CORA.

BSS have been marking your homework – thought you'd
want the results before you start your weekend.

NEIL *and* ZEF. Yes, ma'am. / Thank you, ma'am.

HANNAH. Head of Counter-Terror was on the phone
Wednesday night, saying your system's 'slower than a
Morris Marina'. Hour by hour they were getting so few flags,
they assumed it was broken. Eight-seven per cent behind the
old system.

ZEF *throws* NEIL *an accusing look.* (*'I told you so.'*)

NEIL (*devastated*). Was it that bad?

HANNAH. But. When they cross-checked your flags with their
list of verified targets, you got… drum roll please… (*Grins.*)
All of them. One hundred per cent.

Beat.

ZEF. Seriously?

HANNAH.…with thirty per cent fewer false positives. Plus you're picking up the far-right white nationalists the old system missed: EDL, Combat 18 – all the Nazi bovver-boys.

NEIL. So… it's a success?

HANNAH. Could say that. BSS were straight back on the phone yesterday, eating humble pie and begging me to – (*Reading from her tablet.*) 'set fire to the old system at the earliest opportunity, and replace it with this one.'

NEIL *and* ZEF *share a look of exhausted triumph.*

ZEF. Yes!

HANNAH. But you're not finished yet. We still need a transition plan. You're meeting CIT first thing Monday, then briefing Senior Staff at eleven. That clear?

NEIL *and* ZEF. Yes, ma'am.

HANNAH. Stick around till close of play, make sure it doesn't crash again – then go home, get some sleep. Good work, both of you. Keep it up.

NEIL *and* ZEF. Thank you, ma'am. / Night, ma'am.

HANNAH *exits.* ZEF *jumps to his feet, punching the air,* NEIL *simply smiles –*

ZEF. Get! The hell! In!

NEIL. Thirty-per-cent reduction…

ZEF. It's a triumph!

NEIL (*sceptical*). It's an *improvement*. That still leaves – what? – hundreds of thousands of innocent people, wrongly flagged as –

ZEF. Nope, don't you dare piss on my parade. Barker's happy, Director's happy, we're goddamn heroes – and we're celebrating. Middle Earth marathon at my place, tonight. You, me, *The Lord of the Rings* trilogy – Director's Cut, obviously – and a metric butt-ton of beer.

NEIL. Ah, man, I'd love to, but... I'm seeing Karen.

ZEF's a little crestfallen, but covers it up.

ZEF. Ah. Should've guessed. (*Then.*) Hey, bring her along. Been dying to meet her.

NEIL. Can't, we're... (*Improvising.*) cycling. In the Cotswolds. Mini-break.

ZEF. You're kidding me. You've barely slept for a fortnight, and you want to go *cycling*?

NEIL. Exercise'll do me good. (*Then.*) But look, it doesn't need both of us to keep an eye on this. (*Nods at his screen.*) You head home now, get some sleep – I'll call if I need you.

ZEF. Nah, you're the one with the hot date in Lycra. I'll do the babysitting. You get out of here.

NEIL. You sure?

ZEF. I'm too wired to sleep now, anyway. Go for it.

NEIL. Thanks, mate.

NEIL grabs his bag, starts heading out.

ZEF. Wait – Neil? Before you go, I just... I wanted to say something. (*Hesitates, bashful.*) The past few weeks, building this thing with you... it's been –

NEIL. – a nightmare?

ZEF. A privilege. An absolute bloody privilege. (*Off* NEIL's *look of disbelief.*) No, I mean it. I know I've been bitching and moaning through most of it... threatened to strangle you – several times. But as sleep-deprived and ill and riddled-with-RSI as I feel right now, I've got to tell you: I am so fucking proud. I didn't know I was capable of half the shit we've been doing – and I wouldn't be, if you weren't here bulldozing through every problem I can't solve. I swear, it's like you don't even notice something's hard – you just jump straight to the solution. You're... something special, mate. I'm lucky to work with you.

NEIL walks back to ZEF, visibly moved.

NEIL. You… know I feel the same way, right? You've been incredible –

ZEF. Yeah, yeah, you don't have to say it back – I just wanted you to know. Now get out of here, before I start playing the *Top Gun* theme.

NEIL grins. Gives ZEF a mock-salute.

NEIL. 'You can be my wingman any time.'

ZEF smiles, salutes him back. A warm moment between them. Then –

CORA. Who has two thumbs, and a brand-spanking-new job?

Light's up on CORA's apartment, a bottle of Champagne on the kitchen counter. CORA's dressed up, glowing with pride as NEIL enters.

NEIL. You're kidding…

CORA (*pointing her thumbs at herself*). This fuckin' girl.

NEIL. Yes!

CORA jumps into NEIL's arms, kisses him.

CORA. Deputy Features Editor for the UK's hottest – and only – Kickstarter-funded open-news platform. They'll be bankrupt in six months, but in the meantime, they pay a fucksight more than the *Guardian*.

NEIL. I *told* you you'd smash it.

CORA. Only because you're a bloody psychic. Those practice interview questions – they were *completely* spot on. I mean, it was eerie. The stuff about troll farms, Twitter bots, eroding trust – question after question, I basically had *déjà vu* the entire time. How do you do it?

NEIL. It's not rocket science – just a bit of googling… (*Quickly.*) We're celebrating, right now. Name a restaurant, make it fancy, I'm taking you –

CORA. Oh, no, we're staying right here. I've got pizza, enough Champagne to bathe in – and a few little surprises, to show you exactly how much I appreciate you.

CORA *hands* NEIL *a glass of Champagne.*

NEIL. I like the sound of that.

Lights fade on NEIL *and* CORA, *as they rise on* ZEF – *at his desk in the office, headphones on, dozing. His computer screen projected behind him – a 'trace log' unspooling at incredible speed, line after line, as the new system crunches through data.*

The phone rings on NEIL*'s desk, startling* ZEF *awake. He checks the time. Glares at the phone. Considers ignoring it. Sighs. Picks it up.*

ZEF *(into phone)*. TDSO. *(Beat.)* Nah, he's gone for the weekend... but put 'em through. *(Beat.)* Hello?... No he isn't, but I can take a message... Sorry, which station?... Lost property. You're kidding me, he's left his bike? Poor bastard, must be... Sorry, how long? Three *months*? That's impossible. Describe the bike?... And you're sure it's been there since... No, no, he'll want it back. Thanks for tracking him down, I'll... I'll pass on the message.

ZEF *hangs up, frowning.*

(Under his breath.) How the fuck do you go on a cycling holiday without a bike?

He picks up the phone on his desk, pulls up the contacts app on his computer, finding NEIL*'s mobile number. Dials it.*

(Into phone.) Alright, mate, it's me. Gimme a call when you get this. Cheers.

ZEF *hangs up. Thinks. Pulls up a geolocation programme on his computer... then stops. Weighs his curiosity against the risk of committing a sackable offence.*

(To himself.) Sod it.

ZEF *pastes* NEIL*'s number into the geolocation programme. Hits 'Enter'.*

*A map of England appears, '****Searching...****' superimposed over it. The map zooms in on London – '****Triangulating...****' Zooms in again: a street near Royal Oak. And again, to a specific building: '****11–30 MERRICK COURT****'.*

… ain't the Cotswolds…

ZEF *pulls up a new application: a database query sheet with fields for 'Address,' 'Phone number,' 'Name.' He taps in* **'11-30 MERRICK COURT'**. *Hits 'Enter'.*

A list of around twenty names appears on his screen. ZEF *scans it quickly.*

Well, it's not your mum. (*Spots a name. Stunned.*) Oh no… No, no, no…

He clicks on the name **'CORA PREECE'**. *The system pulls up* CORA*'s passport photo, date of birth, address and other personal details.* ZEF *stares at the photo.*

Oh, you… idiot. You absolute… fucking…

ZEF *types furiously, logging into battery of restricted surveillance tools. Finds the one he's looking for:* **'TARGET #819-658-562. IMEI: 8143213548192. Device active.'**

Gotcha.

ZEF *clicks 'Launch.' He pulls on a chunky pair of headphones. Listens as –*

Lights up on NEIL *and* CORA*, curled up on the sofa – partially clothed, post-coital. Troye Sivan's 'Heaven' playing softly in the background.*

CORA. More Champagne?

They kiss.

NEIL. Don't mind if I do.

ZEF*'s jaw drops in horror, hearing* NEIL*'s voice.*

CORA (*raising her glass*). To my clairvoyant careers adviser, life-coach – and sexy piece of ass. (*Then, sincerely.*) I bloody love… being your girlfriend, Tom.

NEIL. I bloody love being your boyfriend.

They clink glasses. Drink. ZEF *straining to hear.*

CORA *leans in close to* NEIL*, looking into his eyes.*

CORA. You know what? I totally bottled that. I was going to say… I've wanted to say for a while now… I love you. I really do. (*Beat.*) You don't have to say –

NEIL. I love you, too. So much it scares me.

They kiss, long and deep.

ZEF *buries his face in his hands.*

Lights down.

A screen lights up against the back wall – showing a mobile-phone messaging app. 'Zef' at the top of the screen, a picture of his face in a circle. A new message pops up in a bubble at the bottom of the screen:

'*ZEF: Remember where we tested our potato cannon?*'

A new message appears below it, followed by another – a text conversation unfolding.

'*NEIL: Before or after we started using liquid nitrogen?*'

'*ZEF: After. Meet me there on Monday, 6.30 a.m.*'

'*NEIL: Er… OK. Why?*'

'*NEIL: Zef? What's up?*'

No response. The screen fades. We hear the sound of birdsong. The distant rumble of passing cars.

Lights up on ZEF, *standing alone, wrapped up in an overcoat, pacing a little to keep warm. After a few moments –*

NEIL *approaches in an anorak and hoodie, backpack slung over his shoulder, his smartphone in one hand.*

NEIL'*s smartphone screen projects against the back wall – Google Maps, showing a remote field outside Cheltenham.*

Zef?

ZEF (*turning to face him*). Hey.

NEIL. What's with the field trip?

ZEF. Turn your phone off. Put it in your bag. Put the bag by the tree, over there.

NEIL. What's going on?

ZEF. Do it.

NEIL. Okay.

NEIL *does as instructed – traipses away, puts his bag down, walks back.* ZEF *produces two identical Android phones from his pocket. He hands one to* NEIL.

What is this?

ZEF. There's one app installed. Use it.

NEIL *flicks on the phone, its screen now projected on the back wall. The home screen contains only one app – 'Signal', an encrypted messaging app.* NEIL *taps to open it.*

NEIL. What the hell…?

ZEF. Don't talk. Type. And for fuck's sake keep your screen upright.

ZEF *points up at the sky. He doesn't say it but – 'because satellites.'*

ZEF *types and a message bubble appears on* NEIL*'s screen:*

'**SHERLOCK: How was the cycling holiday?**'

NEIL *types a reply, his username displaying as 'MORIARTY':*

'**MORIARTY: Great. What's with the cloak-and-dagger stuff?**'

Their typed conversation plays out against the back wall:

SHERLOCK: '**Must've been tricky. Without a bike.**'

NEIL *looks questioningly at* ZEF, *who keeps typing.*

'**SHERLOCK: You lying piece of shit. "Tom Flowers."**'

NEIL *seems unsteady on his feet for a moment, looking up towards* ZEF, *then back down at the screen. He starts to type:* '***I'm so sorry** – '* then stops. Deletes. Starts again: '***Let me explain** – '* but stops again. ZEF's already typing again –

'***SHERLOCK: Don't bother denying it – I've got the logs, the intercepts, every minute of your dirty weekend. Give me one good reason why I shouldn't give the lot to Internal Security.***'

NEIL *agonises over his reply. Finally types:*

'***MORIARTY: Because we're friends.***'

'***SHERLOCK: Are you fucking insane? Not good enough.***'

'***MORIARTY: I never meant for it to go this far.***'

'***SHERLOCK: Who gives a shit?***'

'***MORIARTY: She was going to kill herself! Because of what we did to her.***'

'***SHERLOCK: Unless she was going to blow up a building, it was none of your business.***'

'***MORIARTY: I should just sit and watch – ?***'

'***SHERLOCK: YES!!!! YES THAT'S EXACTLY WHAT YOU DO. THAT'S LITERALLY WHAT OUR AGENCY FUCKING DOES.***'

ZEF *starts to walk away.* NEIL *calls after him –*

NEIL. Zef, please. I was saving a life –

ZEF. Save it for Internal Security.

NEIL. No. Zef, I'm begging you… Zef? Zef! (*Racks his brain, desperate. Steels himself. Shouts after* ZEF.) The spank bank.

Beat. ZEF *turns.*

ZEF. What?

NEIL. You tell them about this, I'll tell them about your spank bank.

ZEF *strides back towards* NEIL, *fast.*

I don't want to do it, but –

ZEF (*closing in*). Don't even pretend they're the same.

NEIL. – you abused your power, too. For years – I never said a word.

ZEF. You fucking DARE –

ZEF shoves NEIL – harder than he intended. NEIL stumbles back, falls to the ground.

What I did is *nothing* like… I didn't trick anyone, I didn't fuck anyone –

NEIL. You didn't help anyone. At all. Except yourself – to other people's photos –

ZEF. Unbelievable! Trying to high-road me, after what you did? Abusing every tool we have, just to get your scrawny little dick inside her sad little –

NEIL launches himself at ZEF. Tackles him to the ground. They grapple savagely, punching, kneeing, elbowing – the messy but dangerous scuffle of two people untrained in the finer points of combat, but hell-bent on hurting each other.

In the tangle of limbs, NEIL manages to wrestle ZEF into a headlock. ZEF slams his head back – catching NEIL full in the face. As NEIL jolts backwards in pain, ZEF rolls onto his back, trying to wriggle free, but –

NEIL pins ZEF to the ground, straddling his ribcage. Fists raised, blood streaming from his nose, NEIL bellows at ZEF –

NEIL. I LOVE HER.

NEIL lowers his fists.

I fucking love her.

NEIL lets ZEF go – rolling off his chest, slumping to the ground. ZEF slowly clambers to his feet, wincing with pain. Stands over NEIL.

ZEF. End it. Tonight.

ZEF hobbles away – leaving NEIL bleeding in the grass.

Lights up on CORA*'s apartment, all prepared for a romantic evening – candles, wine, chilled music. The kitchen counter piled with fresh ingredients.* CORA*'s in full domestic-goddess mode, an apron protecting her dress as she cooks.*

NEIL *stands, wipes the blood from his nose... and steps through* CORA*'s front door.*

CORA. Hey, lover!

NEIL. Hey...

CORA. Unexpected surprise, seeing you on a school night. How d'you like my fifties-housewife look? Apron and heels, waiting for my... (*Seeing* NEIL*'s bruised face.*) Jesus, what happened to you?

NEIL. It's nothing, I fell off my bike.

CORA. God, that looks awful, do you want some ice?

NEIL. No, no, it's fine.

CORA. Were you swiped by a car, or – ?

NEIL. No, it was my fault. Stupid mistake, just... going too fast.

CORA. Yikes. Well, this'll help. (*Handing him the glass.*) *Ce soir, le chef vous propose* – your favourite: veggie lasagne with all the trimmings.

NEIL. Can I just –

CORA *dips her finger in a pot of sauce on the hob. Puts it in* NEIL*'s mouth.*

CORA. Taste. I used extra chilli this time. (*Before* NEIL *can reply.*) Pretty good, right? For dessert: salted caramel cheesecake, followed by the two of us finding a use for the leftover chocolate sauce. I have a few suggestions.

NEIL. I'm... not staying.

Beat.

CORA. What?

NEIL. I'm going straight back to Bristol.

CORA. Why? Did something happen?

NEIL *takes a breath.*

NEIL. I've been thinking and… I've decided – we should stop seeing each other.

CORA (*not sure whether to laugh*). Good one.

NEIL. I'm not joking. It's been on my mind for weeks and… I can't put it off any longer. I –

CORA. Oh my God, you're serious.

NEIL. I think you're a very special person, but I'm just not in a place right now where I can commit to a long-term –

CORA. What is this, a prepared speech? You sound like a robot –

NEIL (*ploughing on*). – to a long-term relationship. With my promotion, everything happening at work, I need to be putting my career first, not –

CORA. Your promotion was weeks ago.

NEIL. Please can I just… get through this? I might be transferring abroad soon, maybe America, so it wouldn't be right for me to keep leading you on. I never meant for this to get so serious. Honestly, I was only looking for something casual, so…

CORA (*with relief*). I get it. I see what's –

NEIL. – It's my fault completely. You didn't do anything wrong.

CORA. This is because we said the 'L'-word, isn't it? You're freaking out.

NEIL. No, I'm just not in a place where –

CORA. 'Not in a place to commit', you said that. Tom, listen, this is something that happens, okay? Things start to get serious, you start to panic – 'What if it doesn't work out? What if I get hurt?' That's normal. Doesn't make it true –

NEIL. That isn't it, I told you I've given this a lot of –

CORA. You're looking way into the future, seeing all the ways this could go wrong – it's scary, I get it, like… relationship vertigo. And you know what? This might go wrong, in a hundred different ways. But if it does – we'll deal with it, or we won't. But we don't need to break up *now*, just because we *might* break up in the future. (*Moves closer to* NEIL.) Look at me. Take a breath. How about we just… take it day by day?

CORA *reaches for* NEIL, *touches him. For a moment he waivers. Then steps back.*

NEIL. You're not listening to me.

CORA. I am, and I understand –

NEIL. No, you don't understand. At all. (*Then.*) Okay, I didn't want to say this, but… the truth is… I've met someone else.

Beat.

CORA. Since yesterday?

NEIL. No, she… she works in my office. We have a… connection. I think that –

CORA. Bullshit. I don't believe you.

NEIL. Her name's Hannah – (*Correcting himself.*) Anna.

CORA. Which is it, Hannah or Anna?

NEIL. We're both passionate about the same things. Coding. Software architecture. Network security. And I've realised that's important to me – to have someone I can talk to about my work.

CORA. Tom, you're a terrible liar. This is fear talking, nothing else.

NEIL. Why are you making this so –

CORA. – difficult? Because I love you, Tom. And you love me. You're new at this, but trust me, this is not 'everyday', the connection we have… We're *good* for each other. We've been growing together. I promise you, that is precious and it's rare. If you need some space I can give you some space, but I won't give up on this. So why don't you go home, think about how you really feel. And next week, I'll give you a call –

NEIL (*frustrated*). You *can't* –

CORA. I can, and I will. If you don't pick up, that's your choice, but –

NEIL (*frustrated*). Stop it! Just stop. (*Then.*) Alright. Alright. I've been trying to spare you this, but… you're wrong, okay? You're *not* good for me. At all. I don't think… the way you are, I don't think you'd be good for anyone. The drinking, the depression, the endless self-pity, it's toxic. When I picture a future where you… get pregnant, we move in together –

CORA *tries to speak, but* NEIL *talks over her.*

… it's a nightmare to me, honestly. The thought of being trapped with you and all your mental… bullshit. You said it yourself – you're a mess. I've been trying to drag you out of it, but I'm tired of pulling you up. So when I hear all this stuff about how 'precious' and 'rare' this is – how you 'won't give up' on me… Of course you won't. Because a parasite needs a host.

Long pause. CORA *staring at* NEIL, *in shock.*

Your spare key. (*Puts a key on the counter.*) Goodbye, Cora.

NEIL *heads for the door. Opens it. He looks back at* CORA, *who is standing silent, shattered. Opens his mouth to speak…*

… but closes it again. Walks out.

Lights down on CORA*'s apartment.*

Spotlight on NEIL, *standing alone, shaking. A burst of tears hits him, overwhelms him for a moment. But he chokes it back down.*

ZEF. Go on.

Lights up on ZEF *at a cramped table in a café, a laptop open in front of him. The laptop screen projects onto the back wall – windows showing Tom Flowers' Facebook page, Instagram, Twitter, and the fake website for 'Net Vault Tech'.*

NEIL *reluctantly sits next to him. Turning the laptop to face him,* NEIL *clicks into Facebook's settings, selects the 'Delete Account' button. A warning appears:* '**This action cannot be undone. Are you sure?**' *After a moment,* NEIL *clicks:* '**Yes.**'

And the rest.

A few swift clicks, and Tom Flowers is wiped from the internet.

You've gotta purge the internet archive too. And the cached pages on Google.

NEIL. I know. (*Then.*) D'you... want a coffee?

ZEF (*with disdain*). No. I'm not staying. I'll keep your secrets but I'm not your friend.

A beat as they look at one another. A moment of sadness – before ZEF*'s face hardens again. He stands to leave.*

NEIL. She's still a suicide risk. She tried once before.

ZEF. I'll keep an eye on her. Not you.

NEIL. I bet you'll enjoy that.

ZEF (*with venom*). Careful.

ZEF exits. The lights rise on NEIL and ZEF's office, deserted. NEIL steps into the office. Spotlight on DENISE.

DENISE. That's where it ended?

NEIL. Zef rigged our systems with a thousand different alerts around Cora's profile. Shut me out completely. I tried checking her Facebook page using a VPN, but... she'd deleted it. I was cut off.

DENISE. Can't say I blame him.

NEIL. I did, though. Blame him. We... pretty much stopped talking, after that – which is difficult, in a shared office. I wasn't sleeping much. Wasn't really eating. (*Then.*) Have you heard of Stein's Law?

DENISE. No.

NEIL. 'If something can't go on forever, it will stop.'

Lights down on DENISE.

ZEF enters, sits at his desk. Pulls on a pair of headphones and starts working. NEIL has his own headphones on – working on some code.

HANNAH (*off*). Guys, what the hell is this?

HANNAH *sweeps into the office brandishing two folders, agitated*. NEIL *and* ZEF *pull off their headphones*.

CIT have two different hardware lists from us, which completely contradict each other. These are huge requisitions – we can't fuck them around like this. Which one are they supposed to act on?

NEIL (*pointing at one folder*). That one – I sent it in yesterday.

ZEF (*exasperated*). You've gotta be… System planning's *my* job. (*Pointing at the other folder.*) Use that one, I sent it two days ago.

NEIL. How can you 'plan the system' when I'm doing the architecture?

ZEF. The *software* architecture – I'm doing the hardware.

NEIL (*simultaneously*). No, we all agreed – you're on user requirements, I'm on implementation –

ZEF (*simultaneously*). Check your fucking emails – I was always writing the system plan, you're supposed to be –

HANNAH (*interrupting them*). ALRIGHT. That's enough. (*Then.*) What's gotten into you two? First the road-map mess, then the delayed roll-out, now you're wasting – how long, days? Weeks? – duplicating each other's work. You're in the same bloody room! How does this happen?

A silence. ZEF *and* NEIL *won't even look at each other.*

Okay, if you've had a lover's tiff, that's none of my business. But when it affects the work, when it makes us look incompetent – (*Holds up the folders.*) that's something else. Figure this out, *today*, and start acting like professionals, or one of you's getting reassigned.

ZEF. No need. (*Then.*) I'm transferring. Back to NDIS.

HANNAH. What?

ZEF. Put in the request last week. Mike says it's fine – he needs the help –

HANNAH. You didn't think to discuss this with me? Maybe tell me you were –

ZEF *stands abruptly, pushes his keyboard away.*

ZEF (*glaring at* NEIL). Lot of that going around.

ZEF *exits, leaving* HANNAH *gobsmacked. She looks to* NEIL.

HANNAH. What the hell was that?

NEIL. It's… my fault. I'm sorry.

HANNAH. What's your fault? What happened to you two? One minute you're Butch and Sundance, the next you won't even look at each other.

NEIL. He's just angry, because… (*Hesitates, then.*) I'm leaving.

HANNAH. Leaving…?

NEIL. The agency. I'm resigning.

Beat.

HANNAH. *What?*

NEIL. You'll have my resignation letter by this evening.

HANNAH. But you can't… You can't both just –

NEIL. Zef'll stay, if I go. It's better for everyone. So I'm… pursuing some opportunities in the private sector.

HANNAH'*s too stunned to respond for a moment.*

HANNAH. Did I do something to make you feel –

NEIL. No. This is all me – I'm just burnt out. After the crunch.

HANNAH. Then take some holiday. Take a sabbatical for all I care – but don't just desert us, in the middle of building this thing.

NEIL. It's all planned out now. Zef can finish it.

HANNAH. Look, Zef's brilliant, but – (*Checks behind her, makes sure no one's listening.*) he isn't you. If this is about your salary –

NEIL. It's not.

HANNAH. – I'll get you bumped up a grade, it's more than deserved. Whatever the headhunters have offered you –

NEIL. This isn't about money. I've just… lately I've been asking myself… what exactly we do here.

HANNAH. Keep our country safe? Protect people from a thousand different threats. A free society is a beautiful thing, but it's also vulnerable. Fragile. We need the best minds in the country protecting it – and that means people like you.

NEIL. But *how* are we protecting it?

HANNAH. By any means necessary.

NEIL. Suppose our agency, our capabilities, existed fifty years ago. Would the Watergate Scandal have broken?

HANNAH. Probably, since it happened in America.

NEIL. The suffragettes, then. If we'd known every railing they were going to chain themselves to, ahead of time – would they have managed a single successful protest? Or would we have scooped them up pre-emptively, thrown them in jail for conspiracy?

HANNAH. 'We' don't arrest anyone – we gather information.

NEIL. Don't we just. We've hacked half the planet to build a terrorist-detector which doesn't work. But it can detect journalists, like Cora Preece. And dissidents, like Ameera Al-Mansur –

HANNAH. Look, that op was a catastrophe – I know it shook you up. It shook all of us up. But don't paint the whole agency with that brush – the good we do here far, far outweighs the occasional shitty outcome on one isolated operation.

NEIL. Knowing everything you know about what we've built here – do you honestly still believe that?

Pause.

HANNAH. It's been a pleasure working with you, Neil. I wish you every success.

HANNAH *exits.* NEIL *packs his personal items into clear plastic bags. Holding his meagre possessions, he walks out of the office, into –*

– the car park outside Benhall. ZEF's *waiting for him.*

ZEF. Trying to sneak off, without saying anything?

NEIL. Didn't want to make a fuss.

ZEF. Bit late for that.

A pause.

So… what's next for you?

NEIL. Don't know. Haven't really thought about it, to be honest.

ZEF. I reckon you'll land on your feet. The skills you've got, this place on your CV – those big, shiny corporate types'll snap you up.

NEIL. I think I might take a break. Maybe travel or something. Digital detox.

ZEF. 'Neil Dunbar, IRL'? I give it five minutes, tops.

NEIL *smiles, enjoying a tiny scrap of the friendship they used to have. Before it evaporates – leaving only the awkward silence between them.*

NEIL. Zef, listen –

ZEF. Don't do it. No more apologies.

NEIL. Please, just let me say –

ZEF. I know, I know – you're sorry, I'm sorry, it's a sorry situation. Let's not keep raking over it.

NEIL. Then… I don't know what to say.

ZEF. Bye. Mate.

NEIL. Bye.

NEIL *starts to walk away.*

ZEF. Stay out of trouble, yeah? (*Nods towards the main building.*) They'll be keeping an eye on you, for a while.

Standard procedure. Don't be paying any visits to... anyone you shouldn't.

NEIL. I won't.

ZEF. I mean it.

NEIL. I know.

ZEF. That's not why you're doing this? To go back to...

NEIL. Of course not.

ZEF scrutinises NEIL. *Trying to tell whether he's lying. After a moment –*

ZEF. Okay then.

ZEF turns and walks away. NEIL *watches him go.*

Lights up on NEIL*'s bedroom – messier than when we last saw it. A host of electronic devices piled up on his desk – his PC, dozens of hard drives, an assorted collection of laptops, tablets, mobile phones and games consoles – all in varying states of disassembly. A large worktop vice clamped to his desk.*

NEIL *enters his bedroom, chucks down his stuff. Opens a drawer, pulling out a large electric drill with a rotating power-sander tip. He grabs one of the half-disassembled hard drives on his desk, pulls out the platter. Clamps it into the vice. Switches on the drill – the power-sander spinning violently. He presses it against the disc platter, obliterating the surface.*

Spotlight on DENISE.

DENISE (*shouting over the whine of the drill*). Was that really necessary?

NEIL (*over the drill*). Most reliable way to wipe a device – the old-fashioned way. Couldn't use software to zero the drives – they might see it.

DENISE (*over the drill*). But why bother wiping your old devices? What was on them?

NEIL *stops the drill, satisfied.*

NEIL. Fragments of me. Old photos, messages, documents.
I wanted to disappear, get somewhere the agency couldn't
find me. But it's hard to move through this world 'randomly'
– most of us fall back on places we've been before, on
friends, relatives, contacts. The less I leave behind, the
harder I am to find.

NEIL *tosses the platter into a black bin liner, starts shoving
the other electronic devices in as well.*

DENISE. And where were you planning to go?

NEIL. Nowhere, at first. Zef was right, they'd be watching,
I had to be patient. Drew up a list of all the things a 'normal'
ex-employee would do, and worked my way through them.
Emailed recruitment firms, looked at holidays, bought some
video games. Faked ticket purchases for a round-the-world
trip, so I could empty my bank accounts, shift the money
into bitcoin.

NEIL*'s computer screen projects onto the back wall,
windows piling up on the desktop – emails to corporate
IT firms, travel websites, game-purchase pages...*

It got so boring, pretending to be myself, I wrote a Python
script to do it for me: browsing my usual websites at quasi-
random intervals, streaming my favourite shows. I called the
programme 'Real Neil' – it was tragic how few lines of code
it took.

*On screen, a code editor shows the Python code for '**THE
REAL NEIL SIMULATOR**'. The computer begins browsing
websites by itself – Ars Technica, The Register, Hacker News,
Reddit, etc.*

NEIL *starts packing clothes into a backpack. Zips up the
bag. Pulls on a fresh hoodie. Takes a last look at the screen.*

After sixty-two days... I figured I'd probably bored them
into submission.

DENISE. You went on the run.

NEIL *pulls the (large) hood up over his head, obscuring his
features. Leaves his phone on his desk. Steps out of his
bedroom, as the light fades on* DENISE.

Lights up on a table in a bar – the same place NEIL *and* CORA *first met.*

NEIL *pulls back his hood as he enters, the babble of a lunchtime crowd all around him. He picks up two glasses of vodka with orange juice, carries them to the table – looking round for signs of* CORA. *She isn't here. He takes a seat, tossing his backpack at his feet.*

He waits, nervously, eyes on the entrance. Wipes the sweat off his palms, adjusts his appearance. Checks the time. Fidgets. Checks the entrance again. Checks the time again. Fidgets. Finally –

CORA *enters. A little paler than when we last saw her, tired, but made up and dressed up (as you do, when meeting an ex) to present an aura of health and happiness.*

She stops when she catches sight of NEIL. *Takes him in.* NEIL *waves awkwardly, stands up. She glances around at the rest of the bar, then heads for his table.*

NEIL. Hi.

CORA (*wary*). Hello.

NEIL *steps forward to give her a hug – then thinks better of it.*

NEIL. I didn't think you'd come.

CORA. Me neither. (*Holding up a scrap of paper.*) Note under my door. Little bit creepy.

NEIL. Sorry about that, I… didn't know how to… Sorry.

NEIL *sits, expecting* CORA *to do the same. She remains standing.*

I got you a drink.

CORA *looks at the drink, then back at* NEIL. *Sits down.*

CORA. What are you doing here – another conference?

NEIL. No. I… wanted to see you.

A beat.

CORA. Really.

NEIL. Yes.

CORA. Because last time you were here, you said –

NEIL. I know what I –

CORA (*talking over him*). – you said you never wanted to see me again, as long as you lived. You were really quite emphatic on that point.

NEIL. I was an idiot.

CORA. Well, *there's* something we can agree on.

NEIL. That's why I'm here. The only reason I came to London. To apologise.

CORA *takes a swig of her drink. Glares at him.*

CORA. Go on.

NEIL. I... don't expect you to forgive me – what I did was unforgivable.

CORA. Something else we agree on.

NEIL. But I need you to know... what I did that day, what I said... I wasn't myself. I really wasn't.

Beat.

CORA. You weren't yourself.

NEIL. Exactly.

CORA. That's your explanation.

NEIL. That's the start of –

CORA. Who were you, then?

NEIL. I don't mean... I'm just trying to say... I wasn't in my right mind at the time. I was so stressed, under this pressure at work like you wouldn't... pressure I can't even describe to you. And I thought the only way to fix it was to... lash out. Push you away. What I did that day I regret more than anything else in my life. If I could just delete it from the space–time continuum, I would. I'm sorry, Cora, I'm so fucking sorry.

CORA *says nothing. After a moment.*

This was a mistake. I don't know why I thought I could... fix this. You're right not to forgive me. I'm sorry, I won't do this again.

NEIL *stands.*

CORA. Hang on – you're leaving?

NEIL. Isn't that what you want?

CORA. Really, two minutes of grovelling – that's all you've got in you? And when I don't accept your apology immediately, what, you're just giving up? (*Off* NEIL*'s paralysed indecision.*) You really do suck at this, you know that? But I give you points for working the 'space–time continuum' into an apology – not many guys would try that.

NEIL *starts to sit again, but* CORA *stops him –*

Uh-uh, let's not be the kind of people who shake out their shitty laundry in public. How about this: if we were to go back to my place – *just to talk* – do you promise to leave if I ask you to?

NEIL. Of course.

CORA *swigs down the rest of her drink.*

CORA. Then let's go.

She stands, heads for the exit. NEIL *grabs his backpack, pulls up his hoodie, and follows.*

Lights down on the bar.

CORA*'s apartment is in darkness – lights off, windows blacked out. We hear the jangle of keys, the click of a lock turning – and* CORA *and* NEIL*'s voices outside the door.*

(*Off.*) I warn you, it's a bit of a mess.

NEIL (*off*). I don't care.

CORA (*off*). Right answer.

The clunk of another lock. And another.

NEIL (*off*). How many locks do you have?

CORA (*off*). Exactly the right amount.

NEIL (*off*). Did you get burgled or something?

CORA (*off*). No.

Two more locks unlatch, and CORA *opens the door. Clicks on the lights to reveal –*

– an apartment in chaos. Fist-sized holes punched into the plaster of the walls, leaving pipes exposed, electrical wires dangling. The carpet ripped up, holes hacked into the wooden boards beneath. The sofa, too, has holes slashed into it, stuffing spilling out. The windows have been covered by blackout fabric. The bed is gone, replaced with a mattress jammed into one corner. The far wall is obscured by bedsheets, pinned to the plaster.

Every surface is covered with stacks of paper – newspapers, computer printouts, folders, notebooks, yellow legal pads – piled high. The kitchenette is littered with discarded cartons of orange juice, vodka bottles and instant-noodle packets.

NEIL *looks around, dumbstruck by the carnage, as* CORA *closes the front door and begins locking the multiple deadbolts, chains and locks installed on it.*

NEIL. Wow.

CORA. I warned you.

NEIL. What... happened here?

CORA. I made some changes.

CORA*'s carrying a shopping bag with a couple of bottles of wine inside. She clears a space on the kitchenette counter, plonks them down.*

NEIL. Can I ask why?

CORA. Security. (*Then.*) Do you have a phone on you?

NEIL. No, I... forgot to grab it on my way out. Came without it.

CORA (*indicating his backpack*). You got a laptop in there?
    iPad?

NEIL *shakes his head.*

Okay.

CORA *takes out her own mobile phone. Grabs a nearby roll of kitchen foil, tears off a sheet – and wraps her phone in it. Puts the neat foil package into her microwave – her movements matter-of-fact, like this is nothing unusual.* NEIL *stares with mounting concern.*

NEIL. Did you just put your phone in the –

CORA. – microwave, yes.

NEIL. And… why did you – ?

CORA. It's a Faraday Cage, blocks wifi signals. Foil takes care of the rest. (*Then.*) Have a seat. Wine or vodka?

NEIL. Er… wine, thanks. So… you've blacked out your windows, ripped up the carpet… and you keep your phone in the microwave, because…?

CORA*'s sifting through the mess in her kitchen, trying to find a bottle opener.*

CORA. I told you – security. You work in IT, you know all about 'info-sec', right?

NEIL. Of course I do, but –

CORA. Well, now I know about it too. I've been doing some reading, started taking precautions. (*Holding up a bottle opener.*) Found it. (*Starts cutting the foil on the bottle. Glances up at* NEIL.) I see the way you're looking at me. 'Uh-oh, Cora's gone off the deep end.'

NEIL. No, no, it's just… a shock, that's all –

CORA. Wishing you'd never come back?

NEIL. Not for a second. Wishing I'd come sooner.

CORA *laughs.*

CORA. Don't flatter yourself, Casanova – this has nothing to do with you. I'm not depressed, I'm not mentally ill – I'm just a journalist. Trying to do my work. In this fucking country.

So before you go calling the men in white coats… (*Uncorks the wine with a 'pop'.*) consider the alternative. What if I'm completely sane, and these – (*Indicates her flat.*) are simply the times in which I find myself?

CORA *pours the wine – sloppily filling two glasses, right to the brim.*

NEIL. And what times are those?

CORA. A time when the schizophrenics are finally right. When the very thing they've been screaming about for centuries has actually come to pass.

She holds out an over-full glass of wine. NEIL *takes it, warily.*

NEIL. Which is?

CORA (*in a mock-whisper*). 'The government's trying to steal my thoughts.' (*Then.*) Cashews? I'm starving. (*Grabs a bag of cashews. Glances up at* NEIL.) The look on your face. Relax. (*Taps her head.*) No tin-foil hat.

NEIL. Just around your phone.

CORA. Of course. That's how they steal them – my thoughts. (*Opening a bag of cashews.*) And because this country has a gaping hole where a Constitution should be, there's nothing to stop them. Every time I ping an electron down a wire, or whizz a radio wave through the air – there they are, catching the lot.

NEIL. But those are just capabilities – doesn't mean they're doing it to *you*. They're looking for… you know, criminals. Terrorists, paedophiles…

CORA. Ah yes, 'terrorists and paedophiles', the boogeymen of the surveillance state. 'If you've got nothing to hide, you've got nothing to fear' – that's the slogan, right? (*Eating cashews.*) Because only *bad* people pose a threat to the status quo. Bad people like – civil rights activists. Greenpeace. Amnesty International. And, of course: naughty, no-good investigative journalists. Like me. (*Sips her wine. Grimaces.*) Not very cold – would you prefer vodka?

CORA *opens her fridge. Pulls out a vodka bottle – its cap missing, a rag stuffed down the neck instead.*

NEIL. So… you think you're being watched?

CORA. I know I'm being watched. When I talked to Ameera, they were listening. When I talked to Dee, they were watching.

NEIL. You know that for certain?

CORA. I know that for certain.

CORA *turns to face* NEIL. *Opens a kitchen drawer, reaches inside.*

NEIL. How do you know that?

CORA. Because. It was you.

CORA *raises her hand to reveal a Taser.*

NEIL. Wha–

She pulls the trigger.

Two wired darts thwack into NEIL*'s chest, slamming a thousand volts through his body.* NEIL *convulses in agony, spasming in his chair as –*

– CORA yanks the rag out of the vodka bottle (which does not, in fact, contain vodka). She stands over NEIL, *Taser in one hand, soaking rag in the other. She shoves the rag against his face, covering his mouth and nose. Holds it in place.*

Blackout.

End of Act Two.

ACT THREE

Lights up on CORA*'s apartment.*

NEIL *is unconscious in a chair, a chunky ball-gag in his mouth, held in place with thick leather straps buckled around his head. His arms are handcuffed behind his back, his ankles zip-tied to the chair legs.*

CORA *is at the kitchenette counter,* NEIL*'s backpack open in front of her, its contents – clothes, books, shoes, toiletries – strewn across the surface. She's holding a strange-looking electronic device, a black box the size of a walkie-talkie, with a screen and retractable antenna, which she's sweeping over the items from* NEIL*'s bag.*

NEIL *starts to stir – shifting in his restraints, groggy.* CORA *grabs the Taser from the counter. Heads towards* NEIL *as –*

– he awakes with a jolt. Panics. Kicks his legs against the zip-ties, strains his arms, trying to scream through the gag.

CORA. Ah-ah-ah.

She aims the Taser at his chest. NEIL *falls silent, eyes wide.*

You scream, you get zapped – higher voltage this time. Understand?

A beat. NEIL *nods. Whimpers.*

Are you going to keep quiet?

He nods again.

Good.

CORA *heads back to the kitchen counter. Picks up her bug detector.* NEIL *watches – terrified, but no longer struggling.* CORA *continues patiently scanning his possessions – the soles of his shoes, each individual item from his sponge-bag – through what follows.*

Tell me, have you ever heard of the Hawthorne effect?
(*Beat*.) Yes or no – the Hawthorne effect.

NEIL *slowly shakes his head*.

One of the great accidental discoveries of our time. Like
penicillin or... I don't know... microwaves. I'll probably fuck
it up, but the gist of it is: there was this factory called
Hawthorne Works. They made... telephones, I think. Or
widgets of some sort – it's not important. What's important is,
they bring in a business-school professor to run some
experiments, to figure out how to make their workers more
productive. He takes a dozen workers off the assembly line,
puts them in a small room, and he starts... messing with them.

Finished with NEIL*'s possessions,* CORA *walks towards*
NEIL*, bug detector in hand*.

He gives them brighter lights. Dimmer lights. Longer breaks,
shorter breaks. Early lunch, late lunch. You name it, he
tweaks it, to see if they make more widgets. And the results
are... spectacular. But also – baffling.

CORA *starts scanning* NEIL*'s body, passing the antenna
slowly over his limbs*.

You see, these workers in the small room, they're pounding
out widgets like there's no tomorrow. But our clever
professor has no idea *why*. No matter what he does to these
guys – lights, breaks, meals, even stuff that should stress
them out – makes no difference. They're just way, way more
productive than they were before. But he doesn't know how
he did it.

Satisfied that NEIL*'s 'clean', she switches off the detector.
Retracts the antenna*.

I expect you know the answer, though. (*Off* NEIL*'s
bewilderment*.) No? The answer is: the work conditions
didn't matter. The lighting didn't matter, the breaks didn't
matter. What mattered was: (*Slowly*.) the workers in the
small room knew that someone was watching them. And
that, my friend, is the Hawthorne effect: people change their
behaviour, when they know there's someone watching.

CORA *returns to the kitchenette counter. Puts down the bug detector, picks up small cardboard box – an Amazon envelope – and heads back towards* NEIL, *opening the box as she continues.*

So tell me – how have *I* changed, since you started watching me? Do I seem different to you?

Pause. NEIL *doesn't respond.*

What did you see, I wonder? Did you watch me cry? Was that loud enough for your microphones to pick up? Did you type it up in a report somewhere: 'Subject woke up sobbing… Subject cried until she threw up in the sink, then cried because she'd thrown up in the sink…' That sort of thing?

NEIL *doesn't answer.* CORA *removes a plastic case from inside the box.*

Did you watch me getting dressed? In the shower? Did you watch me masturbate?

NEIL *shakes his head.*

Did you get off on it, watching me? Did *you* masturbate?

NEIL *shakes his head again.*

Would you tell me, if you did?

CORA *opens the case, to reveal – a pair of poultry shears. Large, heavy-duty, blades the size of kitchen knives.*

NEIL *panics, shifting in his chair, pulling at his restraints.* CORA *presses the point of the shears to his throat – silencing him instantly.*

If I take off that gag, are you going to scream?

NEIL *shakes his head, carefully.* CORA *moves behind him – keeping the shears to his throat.*

When I take this off, I only want to hear one thing out of your mouth: MI5, MI6, or Saudi Intelligence. No shouting, no begging, no lying – you tell me who you are, and who you work for, or you get hurt. Ready?

NEIL *nods.*

CORA *opens a clip on the ball-gag, which drops to one side of* NEIL*'s head – dangling, gleaming with spittle.* NEIL *gasps for air, works his aching jaw muscles.*

NEIL. Cora, please, please stop –

CORA. Ah-ah-ah – those aren't the rules. Who are you, who sent you?

NEIL. It's me! Nobody sent me, you know me – please can we just –

CORA. Have it your way.

CORA *roughly yanks the gag back across* NEIL*'s mouth.* NEIL*'s shouts of pain are quickly muffled, as the gag clips back into place.*

Let's talk about Tom Flowers, shall we?

CORA *strides towards the far wall. Pulls down the bedsheets covering it, to reveal:*

– dozens of photographs and computer printouts. Screenshots from the 'Net Vault Tech' website, pictures of Bristol, of bike rides – all taken from Tom Flowers' accounts.

Tom Flowers, who works for a company which vanished from the internet, the day after he dumped me. Whose social-media pages – Instagram, Facebook, Twitter – all vanished minutes later. All of them disappearing from Google's cached pages, too, by the end of the day. But not before I'd grabbed some screenshots.

CORA *points at the pictures on the wall, as she continues –*

Tom Flowers, whose company, Net Vault Tech, has a fake address, in a non-existent building in Bristol. And that, I think, is when the bottom really fell out of my existence.

CORA *turns away from the wall, heads back towards* NEIL *– shears in hand.*

The man I loved, the man I daydreamed about spending my life with – didn't exist. He was a liar. Maybe a con-artist? But my overdraft remains untouched. So if it wasn't money, what did Tom Flowers want from me? Sex? There have got to be easier ways to get that.

CORA *circles* NEIL, *watching his reactions closely.*

Then I think about the day you strolled into my life.
Drinking my favourite drink, liking my favourite bands,
buying my favourite breakfast, for fuck's sake. And that's
when I realise – the people who killed my story, and my
career, the people who murdered the mother of a three-year-
old girl… Tom Flowers is one of them.

NEIL *starts struggling in his chair, shaking his head
violently.* CORA *strokes the shears against her fingers.*

'Knowledge is power', that's the old saying, isn't it? Well,
'Tom Flowers' certainly had power over me. Unimaginable,
overwhelming power. And he used that power… to get his
scrawny little rocks off. There's a word for that, Tom – or
whatever your name is. That word… (*Leans in close.*) is
'rape'. So understand this: you invaded my body many, many
times. I have no qualms whatsoever about invading yours.

She steps behind NEIL, *opening the shears.*

In a moment, I'm going to take off that gag. And if the first
thing out of your mouth isn't the full truth about who you
really are, then I'm going to start cutting. (*Scraping the
shears over his hands.*) These filthy little fingers you stuck
inside me. Your limp little rapist's cock. And I'll keep going
from there.

She places the poultry shears around his right thumb. NEIL
struggles, but she yanks back on the handcuffs.

Ready?

CORA *unclips the ball gag.*

NEIL. I was going to tell you

CORA. Well, that's a lie –

CORA *squeezes on the shears.*

NEIL. NEIL DUNBAR! My name is Neil Patrick Dunbar. I'm
twenty-eight years old. I grew up in Putney. I live in
Cheltenham not Bristol, and I worked for… I worked for
GCHQ.

Beat. CORA *steps back from* NEIL, *trembling. Suspicions are one thing, having them confirmed is another.*

CORA. You… fucking bastard.

NEIL. I wanted to tell you –

She clubs NEIL *on the back of his head with the shears' handle.* NEIL *cries out in pain.* CORA *turns away, pacing, fist clenched in fury.*

That's why I came. To tell you. You don't need to hurt me – I *want* to tell you everything.

CORA*'s still pacing, scarcely hearing him.*

I worked there seven years, first in Network Ops, then Info-Sec. My unit, we… investigated national defence leaks. Your articles with what's-his-name, Fergus. They put you on our radar. We wanted the source for your Saudi stories. You led us to Ameera.

CORA *flinches at the mention of* AMEERA*'s name. Picks up the Taser from the kitchenette counter in front of her.*

CORA. So you killed her.

NEIL. No, it wasn't like that – I swear. The leakers my unit caught, they'd get arrested, prosecuted, but not *killed*, that's not how we… I wouldn't work somewhere that did that –

CORA. Then who killed her?

NEIL. I don't know.

CORA. Bullshit.

NEIL. I don't! If I knew, I'd tell you –

CORA. Fuck you.

CORA *points the Taser at* NEIL.

NEIL. No, please –

She pulls the trigger, hits NEIL *with another burst. He jerks in his chair, jaw clenched, rattling his restraints. She turns off the current.* NEIL *sucks in air. Sobs.*

CORA (*approaching with the shears*). Who killed Ameera?

NEIL. I DON'T KNOW. (*Gasping for air.*) On my life, on my family… I don't know… (*Chokes, coughs violently.*) we were literally sent home the day she –

CORA. And you didn't ask? You gave them her name, she shows up dead, you're not even a bit fucking curious?

NEIL. No one tells us anything, that's how it works, everything's… (*Coughs.*) compartmentalised. You want to Tase me, do it. Cut off my fingers, it won't change the truth – I have no idea who killed Ameera. If I knew, I'd tell you. (*Then.*) I'm sorry.

A beat as CORA *digests this*.

CORA. The spreadsheet?

NEIL. We never saw it. The op was shut down. We were reassigned.

CORA. So you stopped watching me?

NEIL. Those were our orders, yes.

CORA (*with venom*). Then why the fuck do you show up *six months later*, in my local, drinking screwdrivers?

NEIL *looks at the ground, shifts in his chair.*

NEIL. For a while after…

CORA (*pushing*). Yes?

NEIL. I kept… checking in on you. From time to time.

CORA. 'Checking in.'

NEIL. To make sure you were okay –

CORA. You were stalking me.

NEIL. I was *worried* about you. Cared about you –

CORA. I don't CARE if you 'cared'! Your motives don't matter here – you *violated* me. The things you must've seen… I can't even… I was in pieces, I did things… disgusting things. Can you imagine how humiliating it is? To know someone was *watching* every moment of –

NEIL. I never judged you –

CORA. *You should never have seen them!* You treated my life like a fucking YouTube channel, and when that wasn't enough, you jumped on a train for the live show.

NEIL. I never would have come here if you hadn't been minutes away from hanging yourself from that beam. You're only alive to judge me because I kept you safe.

Beat.

CORA. And fucking me?

NEIL *hangs his head.*

Was that part of the plan?

NEIL. There was no plan, I was improvising. You keep doing that – implying this was about sex. I came here expecting to find a *corpse* –

CORA (*ignoring him*). You tricked me into bed, fucked me for a few weeks, then threw me away like garbage when you'd had your fill –

NEIL. I never wanted to end it! Someone found out about us – I *had* to end it. But you saw straight through me, you knew I still loved you –

CORA. DON'T use that word. Don't you dare – you don't know what the fuck it means.

Beat.

NEIL. I know it would be easier for you, if that were true. But I do. Love you.

CORA. Fuck off.

NEIL. Why d'you think I'm here? I quit the agency, I've lost my friends, my career –

CORA. Aw, poor Neil – I didn't realise *you* were the real victim…

NEIL. That's not what I'm saying –

CORA. Am I supposed to feel sorry for you?

NEIL. No –

CORA. Grateful? You think, what, I'm just going to forgive you? Go back to the way things were?

NEIL. Look at us. Look at this. (*Indicating the flat.*) There's no going back to who we were. I want to start again – new life, new name, somewhere the agency can't find me. I was hoping… maybe… you might want the same.

CORA (*stunned*). Oh my God. That's your big plan? You think I'm going to run away with you? Skip down the beach in Tahiti, sipping Mai Tais and –

NEIL. Would that be so bad? I don't have to be a spy. You don't have to be a journalist. We could just be… us.

CORA. 'Us'? You're a stranger to me. All I know about you is: you're a liar, and a pervert –

NEIL. I'm not a stranger – you *know me*, Cora. I lied about my name and my job, everything else I ever said to you was the truth. When you wanted to die, I was here – that was me. When you were crying yourself to sleep, I was here – that was me. Filling in job applications, practising interviews, reminding you just how fucking spectacular you truly are – that was me. And if you gave me a single chance to prove that to you… I swear to you, I will never lie to you again. I'll spend every day doing whatever it takes to earn your trust.

Pause. CORA *puts down the Taser. Almost seems to be wavering, when –*

The door buzzer sounds. CORA *and* NEIL *both look at the intercom.*

Who's that?

CORA (*confused*). I don't… it can't be Denise.

NEIL (*horrified*). Why would it be Denise?

CORA. I left her a message while you were… Told her I had the whole story.

NEIL. You did *what*?

CORA. An *encrypted* message, obviously – I'm not stupid, I used Signal. But she's in Greenwich at some conference…

NEIL. Fuck. No. Cora, you didn't…

CORA. This story needs to be told –

'BZZZZ' – the buzzer sounds again.

NEIL. Don't answer it.

CORA. I won't. Probably the postman, anyway – he pushes all the buzzers.

NEIL. We need to get out of here. Right now. You sent a message, they've seen it, they'll send someone –

CORA. I told you – it's encrypted –

NEIL. Doesn't matter – *Denise's* phone is… (*Exasperated, impatient.*) Encryption's irrelevant if the end point is compromised. (*Gives up trying to explain.*) Get out, now – the back stairs, run, don't come back.

CORA. Don't overreact, there's nobody –

A loud knock on the door. CORA's head whips round towards it – then back to NEIL.

NEIL (*softly*). Hide.

CORA shakes her head at NEIL. Grabs the Taser.

CORA. Wh… who is it?

A man's voice from outside the door –

MAN (*off*). Cora? It's Fergus. Denise sent me.

CORA looks at NEIL. Shakes her head.

CORA (*whispers*). That isn't Fergus.

NEIL (*softly*). Go out a window. Climb down. Get out.

MAN (*off*). Can I come in?

CORA (*calling*). Give me a second I'm… not decent.

NEIL (*whispering urgently*). WINDOW. GO.

CORA. What about you?

NEIL. Leave me.

CORA shakes her head. Grabs the keys to the handcuffs from the kitchenette counter. Puts down the Taser and starts trying to unlock NEIL's cuffs. It's fiddly, she's shaking with adrenaline –

(*Whispering.*) There isn't time. I'll be fine. GO.

CORA drops the keys.

CORA. Fuckit.

MAN (*off*). Is someone there with you? (*Pounds on the door – THUD-THUD-THUD.*) Cora, open the door. You're in danger.

CORA abandons the handcuffs, points the Taser at the door.

CORA (*calling*). Whoever you are, you can fuck off – I'm armed, I've called the police, they'll be here any minute.

NEIL. No, no, no –

CRACK – a black metal tube slams through the middle of the door, splintering the wood, punching a hole the size of a dinner plate.

Before CORA can react – a black canister flies through the hole...

... clatters across the floor...

NEIL. NO –

– – BANG! – –

A deafening blast... a blinding flash of white magnesium light...

Blackout.

Lights up on NEIL, sitting at a metal table, under harsh white lights.

He looks broken – head slumped, eyes hollow, hair matted with dried sweat. Wearing a pale tracksuit, the top filthy, stained. He doesn't even look up when –

– HANNAH enters. A tablet computer in one hand, a can of Coke in the other.

She stands for a moment, taking in NEIL's hunched, pitiful appearance.

HANNAH. Neil.

NEIL slowly raises his head. Looks at HANNAH. Then back down at the table.

Thirsty?

NEIL doesn't respond. HANNAH approaches.

You look tired. These IS boys don't piss about, do they?

NEIL says nothing.

From what they tell me, you've missed your calling. (*Sits opposite NEIL.*) Should've worked for MI6, the way you stand up to interrogation. (*Nodding towards the door.*) Usually only takes them a few hours, to crack someone. Three days... (*Whistles.*) You can be proud of that.

NEIL says nothing.

Well, I'll say this for you: when you fuck up, you don't fuck about. We've had rogue staff before, but this... (*Leans back, takes a breath.*) Wow.

NEIL tries to speak – but only makes a dry croaking sound. He coughs. Swallows. Tries again – his voice cracked, harsh –

NEIL. Where's Cora? (*Takes a breath.*) They won't tell me.

HANNAH. We'll get to that.

HANNAH pushes the Coke can across the table.

NEIL reaches for it with trembling hands. Tries to open it, but fails, feebly clicking the ring pull.

HANNAH takes the can, opens it. Slides it back to NEIL – who gulps it down.

You see, Neil, you've fucked up on such a thermonuclear scale, we literally don't know what do with you. We know what we *should* be doing – prosecuting you for about a thousand breaches of the Official Secrets Act. But if we did that, we'd have to tell people what you actually did. At which point, we might as well stuff The Doughnut with dynamite and blow the whole agency sky high – because the press will bury us.

NEIL. Tell me what happened to Cora. I don't care what you do to me.

HANNAH. Good. That makes two of us. But whatever we decide, of this you should be in no doubt: (*Coldly.*) we own you. From this day, for the rest of your natural life. And there is no way in hell that you ever touch a computer keyboard, a smartphone, a fucking fax machine, ever again. And believe me, we'll be watching. Listening. And not just us – BSS, too. You're about to become the most surveilled man in this United Kingdom. Which, after what you did, only seems fair. Don't you think?

NEIL *looks down at the table.*

We've got a mountain of papers for you to sign. Whenever you're ready.

NEIL. Cora. I'm not signing anything, till you tell me where she is.

HANNAH *looks at* NEIL *with a pained expression.*

HANNAH. Then you'll sign?

NEIL. Then I'll sign.

HANNAH *considers this a moment. Makes a decision.*

HANNAH. Alright. She was brought in for questioning, same as you. Surprisingly keen to protect you, given what you did to her. But, after a very long night, she gave it all up. You, 'Tom Flowers', the whole miserable mess.

NEIL. Good.

HANNAH. Still needed to keep her quiet, of course, but they're good at that. Found a weak point: turns out her dad's been fiddling his taxes for years. So, a few well-placed threats – she ever talks, Dad goes to prison – and she signed a gagging order. After that, there was no reason to hold her.

NEIL. So… she's out? Thank God…

HANNAH. Listen to me, Neil – I need you to be crystal clear on this. Cora Preece was released without charge. No punishment, no reprisals.

NEIL *sits back in his chair, relieved.*

So this… (*Stands. Slides the tablet towards* NEIL.) This was all her.

NEIL *looks up at* HANNAH, *wary. Then reaches for the tablet.*

I'll give you some time.

HANNAH *heads for the door. Looks back at* NEIL, *struggling to turn on the tablet with his trembling fingers.*

HANNAH *shakes her head. Exits.*

NEIL *manages to unlock the tablet – its screen displaying against the back wall. A news website, a picture of* CORA's *smiling face, beside a photograph of Waterloo Bridge.* NEIL *scrolls up to the headline:*

'JOURNALIST'S SUICIDE "A TRAGIC LOSS"'

NEIL *crumples, as if punched.*

NEIL (*softly*). No.

*The article unspools down the page – '… **body of Cora Preece, journalist and editor at thebuzz.com, was pulled from the River Thames last night… young writer, described by colleagues as "fearless" and "passionate"… reports that Ms. Preece had made previous attempts on her own life…**'*

NEIL *falls apart. Rocks in his chair. Shoves the tablet aside. Buries his head in his hands.*

NO.

In a fit of fury, he grabs the tablet – raises it above his head, about to smash it against the table –

Lights down.

Darkness.

A computer cursor blips to life, projected against the back wall. Spotlight on DENISE.

DENISE. Are you there? (*Then.*) Hello – are you still there?

The cursor zips across, typing out her words – 'Are you there? Hello – are you still there?'

Spotlight on NEIL, *in jeans and a hoodie.*

NEIL. I'm here.

The cursor types out his words. Through what follows (as at the start of the play) their words are projected against the back wall.

DENISE. I was at a conference. When she called me.

NEIL. I know.

DENISE. 'Safeguarding Journalists and their Sources.' (*Then.*) When I saw she was calling, I ignored it. Saw she'd left a voice message, but I didn't... (*Pauses. The cursor hangs, mid-sentence.*) even listen to it. Not for hours. Looked at my phone and thought – 'Sorry, Cora, I can't deal with your madness right now.' And I went about my day. If I'd picked up –

NEIL. It wouldn't have made a difference.

DENISE. It might. (*Then.*) Do you believe them? Was it suicide?

NEIL. I don't know.

DENISE. Did they kill her, Neil?

NEIL. I killed her. (*Hesitates, then.*) However she went off that bridge... it was my fault.

A pause.

DENISE. So... where are you now?

NEIL. Purgatory.

DENISE. But where are you – geographically?

NEIL. London. I work for... (*A melancholy smile.*) the Royal Parks. Assistant On-Site Inspector for the Central Mapping

Team. I drive around in a van, which I assume they've
bugged. I have a clipboard and a pencil, and I… check the
trees are where the map says they are.

DENISE. Wow.

NEIL. No computer, no phone, just like they promised. There's
someone following me – usually two of them – wherever
I go. I live in a bedsit, which I assume is bugged too.

DENISE. Then… how are you communicating right now?

NEIL. It's not very glamorous. (*Then.*) I'm in a tool shed.

*Dim lights rise on a dusty horticultural shed. Landscaping
equipment – shovels, shears, leaf-blowers – strewn across
shelves and hooks along the walls. An improvised desk –
a couple of planks laid across trestles – with sacks of wood-
chippings stacked beside it, to form a makeshift seat.*

NEIL *steps into it, sitting on the pile of wood-chip bags.*

I do the inventory here twice a month. It's small enough that
no one can follow me in. With the lights off, they can't see
me either. The last private place left in my life.

DENISE. And you've got a computer in there?

NEIL. I wish.

NEIL *picks something off the table – a battered smartphone
with a cracked screen.*

One of the landscapers left a knackered old Android phone,
never came back for it. I stole a SIM card from Sainsbury's.
That's when I made contact.

DENISE *hesitates a moment, before –*

DENISE. Is there any way we can meet?

NEIL. None whatsoever.

DENISE. I want to run this story, Neil, but I need proof you are
who you say you are. I need those files.

NEIL. Thomas Henry Hurd, died 1895. St Mary's Church,
Boddington.

DENISE. Sorry?

NEIL. The back of the tombstone, church-side, dig down about a foot. You'll find a metal box, with three high-capacity USB sticks inside. Every one full of thousands and thousands of agency files – everything I could smuggle out.

DENISE. How did you manage that, without a computer?

NEIL. An insurance policy, when I left the agency. In case they came after me later. I stitched USB microdrives behind my belt buckle to get them past the metal detectors. Harvested everything I could. On the red USB stick, you'll find the Al-Mansur files, in a folder called… (*Hesitates*) 'Cora'.

DENISE. I don't know what to say.

NEIL. Just promise you'll publish them.

DENISE. If they check out –

NEIL. They will.

DENISE. Then of course we'll publish. But you do realise… this story doesn't necessarily reflect well on you? You'll be vilified, by all sides.

NEIL. They can't hate me more than I hate myself. (*Pause*.) I went to the bridge where she… (*Can't finish the sentence*.) More than once, I went back there. Even climbed the railing, the last time. And whoever was following me that night – I think they were in a car at the end of the bridge – they stayed back, didn't try to stop me. They just turned off their headlights and waited. Quite content to watch me die. (*Pause*.) So I looked at that car. Thought about whoever was inside it. And I just thought… 'Fuck you.' I'm not going to make this easy. If I'm going to destroy myself… at least I can make it mean something. (*Pause, then*.) Stories like this need to be told. While it's still possible to tell them.

A pause. Then –

DENISE. And if it isn't?

Beat. NEIL *looks confused*.

NEIL. What?

The spotlight on DENISE *flickers. Another voice merging with hers.*

DENISE (*simultaneously*). If it isn't possible to tell them?

HANNAH (*simultaneously*). If it isn't possible to tell them?

NEIL. What do you mean?

The spotlight on DENISE *flickers in sync with another spotlight –*

– over HANNAH, *sitting at a computer.*

The light on DENISE *goes dark. The light on* HANNAH *stays on.*

HANNAH. I wish you hadn't done this, Neil. I truly, truly do.

The cursor continues typing out the words – HANNAH*'s words – in white text.*

NEIL. Denise?

HANNAH. No.

Beat. A grim realisation dawning on NEIL.

NEIL. Who?

HANNAH. Does it matter?

NEIL *looks down. Breathes. Types –*

NEIL. How?

HANNAH. Encryption is irrelevant if the endpoint is compromised.

NEIL *looks down at the phone. Turns it over in his trembling hands. Types –*

NEIL. What happens now?

HANNAH. You'll see.

NEIL. Protecting something beautiful?

HANNAH. By any means necessary.

NEIL *glances towards the door – considers running. But turns back to the phone.*

NEIL. I can tell you how that ends. I've seen it. Every step makes sense, every action seems justified. But before long... you're not who you were. And the beautiful thing you want to protect – is dead.

A thud from outside the tool shed. Someone trying to open the door.

And you're the one who killed it.

A loud thump rattles the tool shed door. Violent, unstoppable.

NEIL *looks up.*

Blackout.